FOWL PLAY

A CHICKEN LOVER'S COOKBOOK

by Judie Rawson

the Best Sellers
Publishing Company

EZ Cookin' Book Series

To My Mimi,

A very special lady —
For the many years that
you have dedicated your
life to me.

With love and
appreciation from
your daughter.

Judie

First Edition
Printed in U.S.A.
First Printing, October 1986

Copyright© 1986 The Best Sellers
All rights reserved
Illustrations by Phyllis Pyle-Gettig

Published By:
  The Best Sellers Publishing Co.
  (under imprint of) EZ Cookin' Book Co.
  9925 Currant Ave.
  Fountain Valley, CA 92708

ISBN: 0-937545-01-5

Library of Congress Cataloging in
  Publication Data

Dear Chicken Lovers,

I have had so much fun with these chicken recipes that I wanted to share them with all of my friends. Unlike the good ole' days when your best friend wouldn't even sell you her favorite family recipe.

We are fortunate today that chicken is not only economical, but also very nutritional. This enables us to serve it every day and not just for Sunday Company.

I'm sure you will have as much fun as I have had with my recipes. There are so many ways to prepare chicken and the majority of them are very simple and use basic ingredients.

Love, Judie

When in the kitchen and you are making a fuss, just choose a recipe and think of us.

The Girls

Chicken Coquette is a "Flirtatious Hen"

Tough chickens come from hard boiled eggs.

ORDER FORM:

To order additional copies send $7.95 (includes shipping and postage. California residents add 6% tax), along with your NAME & ADDRESS to:

FOWL PLAY
c/o THE BEST SELLERS PUBLISHING CO.
9925 CURRANT AVE.
FOUNTAIN VALLEY, CA 92708
(714) 968-9102

NOTE: If you wish a book sent to someone, please indicate their name and address along with yours.

TABLE OF CONTENTS:

How do chickens dance?
"Chick to Chick"

What do you call a greasy chicken?
"A Slick Chick"

2 chicken breasts, cut lengthwise, boned and skinned
¼ cup butter
2 tbsp. chopped parsley
1 tsp. onion salt
Butter - melted
Seasoned salt
Paprika

1. Pound chicken until ¼" thick. Cut butter lengthwise into 4 sections. Place 1 piece of butter at narrow end of each chicken breast. Sprinkle with parsley and onion salt. Fold over sides to cover butter. Roll up in jellyroll fashion, starting at butter end. Refrigerate for ½ hour.
2. Cut into bite-size pieces and secure with toothpicks. Place in baking dish. Brush with melted butter. Sprinkle with seasoned salt and paprika. Cover with waxed paper.
3. Microwave on High for 3 - 4 minutes. Allow to stand 3 minutes before serving.

Bites of pleasure

CHICKEN KIEV

"BREASTS"

Makes 28

**Preparation Time:
½ Hour
Cooking Time:
4 Minutes**

MY CHICKEN SCRATCHES:

_____

_____

_____

_____

_____

CHICKEN PANNE'

"BREASTS"

Appetizers

Serves 8 - 10

Cooking Time: 15 Minutes

MY CHICKEN SCRATCHES:

_____

_____

_____

_____

4 chicken breasts, split, skinned and boned
2 eggs
¾ cup ground almonds
2 cups bread crumbs
2 tsp. grated lemon peel
2 cloves garlic
Olive oil for frying

Sauce:
¼ cup olive oil
¼ cup lemon juice
2 tbsp. parsley, chopped

1. Place chicken breasts between layers of foil and flatten to ¼". Cut into long, narrow, strips, approximately 1¼" wide.
2. Beat eggs in shallow bowl and combine almonds, bread crumbs and lemon peel in another bowl. Dip each chicken strip into the egg mixture first and then into crumb mixture.
3. Heat garlic in enough oil to cover bottom of skillet. When garlic is lightly browned, remove and discard. Fry chicken strips, a few at a time, until light brown (this takes only minutes - as soon as the crumb coating is golden brown, the chicken should be cooked through).
4. Drain on paper towels and serve immediately.
5. Combine oil, lemon juice and parsley. Mix well for sauce to pour over strips.

10 chicken wings
⅔ cup flour, sifted
½ tsp. salt
¼ tsp. pepper
1 egg, beaten
Oil for deep frying

Preheat oil to 325 F.
1. Cut wings in 3 sections (or leave wings in one piece and tuck wing tips under end of bone in first joint).
2. Mix flour, salt and pepper. Dip wings, one at a time into egg. Allow excess to drip off, then roll in flour mixture to coat.
3. Heat oil, about 1 ½" deep to 325 F. Fry wings until golden brown, about 8 minutes, turning once. Drain well on paper towels. Serve with "Dipping Sauce."

"Dipping Sauce"

¼ cup soy sauce
¼ cup sherry or sake
2 tbsp. sugar

1. Combine all ingredients in saucepan.
2. Heat until sugar dissolves.

Appetizers

Makes 30 Pieces

**Cooking Time:
10 Minutes**

MY CHICKEN SCRATCHES:

MEXICAN CHICKEN APPETIZERS

"PARTS 'N PIECES"

Appetizers

Makes 32 Pieces

**Cooking Time:
30 Minutes**

MY CHICKEN SCRATCHES:

_____

_____

_____

_____

_____

2 cups chicken, cooked and shredded
⅔ cup picante sauce
½ cup green onion, sliced
¾ tsp. ground cumin (optional)
Vegetable oil
32 corn tortillas (6 inch)
2 cups Cheddar or Monterey Jack cheese, shredded (8 oz.)
1 large ripe avocado, peeled and mashed
3 tbsp. picante sauce
1 tsp. lemon juice

Preheat oven to 400 F.
1. Combine chicken, picante sauce, onion and cumin. Mix well.
2. Heat about ½" oil in small skillet until hot but not smoking. Quickly fry tortillas in oil to soften, about 5 seconds on each side. Drain on paper towels.
3. Spoon 1 tbsp. chicken mixture and 1 tbsp. cheese down center of each tortilla. Roll tightly. Secure with a toothpick. Place seam down on baking sheet.
4. Bake 400 F. for 18 - 20 minutes or until crisp. Serve warm with Guacamole and add additional picante sauce.

To make Guacamole: Combine avocado, picante sauce and lemon juice. Mix well. Makes about 1 cup. (Avocado pit left in sauce keeps sauce from turning color. Remove when ready to serve.)

1 lb. chicken livers
2 tbsp. onion, finely chopped
2 tbsp. celery, finely chopped
1 cup water
½ cup butter, softened
2 tbsp. dry sherry
¼ tsp. salt
½ tsp. dry mustard
¼ tsp. marjoram
¼ tsp. hot pepper sauce

1. Pierce chicken livers. Combine livers, onions, celery and water in a 1 quart casserole. Cover with a tight fitting lid or plastic wrap. Microwave on medium for 18 - 20 minutes or until tender. Stir halfway through cooking. Drain.
2. Place liver mixture into a blender. Mix until smooth. Add butter and remaining ingredients. Blend well.
3. Spoon into a well greased 2 cup mold. Refrigerate until chilled and firm. Turn onto a serving plate. Garnish with chopped hard boiled egg yolks and parsley.

PARTY LIVER PATE

"LIVERS"

Appetizers

Makes 2 Cups

Cooking Time:
20 Minutes

MY CHICKEN SCRATCHES:

_____
_____
_____
_____
_____

SILVER PAPER CHICKEN

"PARTS 'N PIECES"

Appetizers

Makes 24-32 Pieces

**Preparation Time:
2 Hours
Cooking Time:
20 Minutes**

MY CHICKEN SCRATCHES:

_____
_____
_____
_____
_____
_____

1 chicken, deboned and raw (chicken breasts
   are best for this)
4 tbsp. hoisin sauce
½ tsp. five spice powder
¼ cup sesame oil
3 tbsp. peanut oil
1 clove garlic, crushed
6 fresh cilantro leaves, chopped
2 tbsp. flour
24 to 32 4"x4" pieces of foil
Oil for deep frying

Preheat oil to 375 F.
1. Cut chicken in bite-size pieces. Combine remaining ingredients in mixing bowl and marinate chicken pieces at least two hours.
2. Place each piece of chicken on foil square, wrap loosely, but seal well.
3. Heat oil to 375 F. Deep fry chicken packages a few at a time for 2 -3 minutes. Carefully remove from hot oil with a slotted spoon. Drain on a paper towel.

WAIKIKI CHICKEN SPREAD

1 can chicken (5 oz.)
¼ cup bacon, cooked and crumbled
¼ cup crushed pineapple, lightly drained
¼ cup walnuts or pecans, chopped
2 tbsp. mayonnaise
Dash of pepper

1. Combine all ingredients and mix well.
2. Spread on dry crisp crackers.

CHICKEN TANGO DIP

1 can chicken spread (5 oz.)
1 cup sour cream
¼ cup mayonnaise
⅓ cup walnuts, finely chopped
2 tsp. instant coffee

⅛ tsp. salt
¼ tsp. pepper
1 tsp. lemon juice
Paprika

1. Combine all ingredients in a medium bowl. Stir until well blended.
2. Chill for several hours. Sprinkle with paprika. Serve with crisp vegetables, potato chips or crackers.

MY CHICKEN SCRATCHES:

_____
_____
_____
_____
_____

Makes 24 Pieces

**Cooking Time:
20-40 Minutes**

MY CHICKEN SCRATCHES:

_____

_____

_____

_____

_____

WINGS 'N DRUMMETTES

¼ cup butter
⅓ cup cornflake crumbs
1 tbsp. toasted almonds,
   finely chopped

¼ tsp. salt
¼ tsp. curry powder
24 wing drummettes

Preheat oven to 375 F.
1. Melt butter in saucepan or skillet. Mix cornflake crumbs, almonds, salt and curry powder and place on a sheet of waxed paper.
2. Dip drummettes, one at a time, into butter and allow excess to drip off then roll in crumb mixture. Arrange in single layer on shallow greased baking sheet.
3. Bake 375 F. for 40 minutes or until chicken is tender.

JAMAICAN CHICKEN STICKS

12 chicken wings, cut in half
4 tbsp. dark rum
1 cup seasoned bread crumbs

3 tbsp. butter
Salt and pepper

1. Place wings in shallow pan and drizzle with rum. Cover. Chill for several hours, turning once or twice.
2. Roll wings in bread crumbs, coating well. Saute in butter for 18-20 minutes.

¼ cup butter, melted
¼ cup orange juice
¼ cup light rum
1 garlic clove
¼ tsp. salt
⅛ tsp. ginger
⅛ tsp. pepper
1 chicken, cut up

Preheat oven to 350 F.
1. Combine all ingredients.
2. Brush on chicken. Arrange, skin side up, on cookie sheet. Baste.
3. Bake 350 F. for 1 hour until golden and tender.

How do chickens dance???
"Chick to Chick"

"PARTS 'N PIECES"

Baked

Serves 4

Cooking Time:
1 Hour

MY CHICKEN SCRATCHES:

CRISPY SESAME CHICKEN

"PARTS 'N PIECES"

Baked

Serves 4

**Preparation Time:
30 Minutes
Cooking Time:
1 Hour**

MY CHICKEN SCRATCHES:

_____

_____

_____

_____

1 chicken, cut up
½ cup milk
1 egg, beaten
½ cup flour
1 tsp. salt
¼ cup sesame seeds
Dash of pepper
Margarine - melted

Preheat oven to 375 F.
1. Dip chicken in combined milk and egg. Coat with combined flour and seasonings. Dip in milk mixture again. Coat with flour mixture again.
2. Place in 9"x13" baking dish. Allow chicken coating to dry at room temperature for 15 minutes before baking. (Important)
3. Drizzle margarine over chicken. Bake 375 F. for 1 hour or until tender.

1 cup dry bread crumbs
½ cup grated Parmesan cheese
½ tsp. paprika
¼ tsp. garlic salt
¼ tsp. pepper
1 tbsp. chopped parsley
4 tbsp. butter
1 chicken, cut up

Tough chickens come from hard boiled eggs.

Preheat oven to 350 F.

1. In bowl, stir together bread crumbs, cheese, paprika, garlic salt, pepper and parsley.
2. In a skillet, melt butter. Dip chicken in butter, then roll in crumb mixture.
3. Place chicken, skin side up in a lightly greased baking dish, not touching.
4. Bake 350 F. for 1 hour or until tender. Serve hot or cold. If serving cold, cover and refrigerate for at least 4 hours or overnight.

CRUSTY PARMESAN CHICKEN

"PARTS 'N PIECES"

Baked

Serves 4 - 5

Cooking Time: 1 Hour

MY CHICKEN SCRATCHES:

_____

_____

_____

_____

_____

CURRY CHICKEN DELIGHT

"BREASTS"

Baked

Serves 4

Cooking Time:
1 Hour

MY CHICKEN SCRATCHES:

_____

_____

_____

_____

4 chicken breasts, split, skinned and boned
⅓ cup flour
4 slices bacon
¼ cup honey
2 tbsp. prepared mustard
¼ tsp. salt
½ tsp. curry powder
Hot cooked rice

My Favorite Brother-In-Laws Favorite!

Preheat oven to 350 F.
1. Rinse chicken. Pat dry with paper towels. Coat chicken pieces with flour.
2. In a skillet, cook bacon until crisp. Drain bacon, crumble and set aside. Reserve drippings. Add chicken to skillet, slowly brown on all sides in hot drippings, about 10 minutes. Transfer to 8 x 8" baking pan.
3. Bake chicken, uncovered 350 F. for 30 minutes.
4. Combine honey, mustard, salt and curry powder. Drizzle over chicken. Bake uncovered 15 minutes more. Top with crumbled bacon. Serve with hot rice.

½ cup butter or margarine
1 chicken, cut up
1 can beer
½ tsp. garlic powder
½ tsp. salt
¼ tsp. pepper

Preheat oven to 375 F.
1. Melt butter in baking dish and dredge chicken in butter.
2. Lay skin side up in baking dish. Pour beer over chicken. Sprinkle with garlic powder, salt and pepper.
3. Bake uncovered at 375 F. for 1 ¼ hours.

Delicious served with rice, using sauce from baked chicken.

A Perfect Ending to a Perfect Day

DRUNK CHICKEN

"PARTS 'N PIECES"

Baked

Serves 4

**Cooking Time:
1 ¼ Hours**

MY CHICKEN SCRATCHES:

_____
_____
_____
_____
_____

GOLDEN FLAKE CHICKEN

"PARTS 'N PIECES"

Baked

Serves 8

Cooking Time:
1 ½ Hours

MY CHICKEN SCRATCHES:

_____

_____

_____

_____

_____

⅔ cup evaporated milk
½ tsp. salt
1 tsp. mixed Italian herbs
⅛ tsp. pepper
1 ½ cups instant mashed potato flakes
2 chickens, cut up

Sauce
¼ cup evaporated milk
1 can chicken gravy

All My Men Love This!

Preheat oven to 350 F.
1. Pour milk into pie plate. Stir in salt, herbs and pepper.
2. Empty potato flakes into second plate. Dip chicken into milk mixture, then into flakes to coat well.
3. Place in single layer on ungreased cookie sheet. Bake 350 F. for 1 ½ hours.
4. To make the sauce, blend evaporated milk and gravy in a saucepan. Heat slowly, stir constantly until bubbly, hot and smooth.

3 cups rice crispies, crumbled
1 tsp. paprika
¼ tsp. salt
¼ tsp. pepper
1 chicken, cut up
½ cup mayonnaise

Preheat oven to 425 F.
1. Place rice crispies, paprika, salt and pepper in large plastic bag. Shake to blend well.
2. Brush chicken on all sides with mayonnaise. Place one piece at a time in bag. Shake to coat well.
3. Place on rack in broiler pan. Bake 425 F. for 40-45 minutes until golden brown and tender.

What do you call a greasy chicken?
"" "A Slick Chick""

MOIST 'N CRISPY CHICKEN

"PARTS 'N PIECES"

Baked

Serves 4 - 6

**Cooking Time:
45 Minutes**

MY CHICKEN SCRATCHES:

_____

_____

_____

_____

_____

_____

PECAN CHICKEN DIJON

"BREASTS"

Baked

Serves 4

**Cooking Time:
30 Minutes**

MY CHICKEN SCRATCHES:

_____

_____

_____

_____

_____

2 chicken breasts, split, skinned and boned
12 tbsp. butter
4 tbsp. Dijon mustard
6 oz. pecans, finely ground
2 tbsp. safflower oil
⅔ cup sour cream
½ tsp. salt
¼ tsp. finely ground pepper

Be Daring. "Dahling"

Preheat oven to 350 F.
1. Pound chicken to ¼" thickness. In small saucepan, melt 8 tbsp. butter and add 3 tbsp. mustard.
2. Place pecans in shallow dish. Dip chicken, one at a time, first in butter-mustard then in pecans. Coat thoroughly.
3. In large frying pan, place remaining butter, add oil and heat. Add chicken and saute 3 minutes on each side or until brown. Remove to baking dish and bake 350 F. for 20 minutes.
4. Drain fry pan and deglaze with sour cream. Add remaining mustard, salt and pepper. For each serving, place sauce from fry pan on serving plate, then place chicken on sauce to serve.

¾ tsp. white pepper
½ tsp. ground ginger
½ tsp. cinnamon
¼ tsp. ground cloves
1 whole chicken
¼ cup soy sauce
2 tbsp. honey
½ cup plum jelly
2 tsp. sugar
2 tsp. vinegar
¼ cup chutney

Preheat oven to 350 F.

1. In small dish, mix together pepper, ginger, cinnamon and cloves. Brush inside of chicken with half of the spices. Stir 1 tbsp. soy sauce into remaining spices and brush outside of chicken.
2. Place in refrigerator and let stand 1 hour. Place chicken breast side up on rack in wok over 2" boiling water. Cover and steam for 1 hour.
3. Remove chicken and place in shallow baking pan. Bake 350 F. for 15 minutes.
4. In dish, mix remaining soy sauce and honey, brush on chicken. Mix together jelly, sugar, vinegar and chutney. Brush on chicken. Bake 450 F. for 10 minutes until brown.

PLUM SWEET & SPICY CHICKEN

"WHOLE"

Baked

Serves 4

**Preparation Time:
1 Hour
Cooking Time:
1 Hour 30 Minutes**

MY CHICKEN SCRATCHES:

_____

_____

_____

_____

_____

RED CHILI CHICKEN

"PARTS 'N PIECES"

Baked

Serves 4 - 5

**Cooking Time:
45 Minutes**

MY CHICKEN SCRATCHES:

_____

_____

_____

_____

_____

1 chicken, cut up
Flour
½ tsp. salt
½ tsp. pepper
Oil for frying
1 onion, chopped
1 can tomatoes (1 lb.)
1 can red chili sauce (10 oz.)
Hot cooked rice or noodles

Cold Night Hot Chick!

Preheat oven to 350 F.
1. Coat chicken pieces with seasoned flour and brown on all sides in oil in large skillet. Transfer browned chicken to a casserole. Pour out most of the oil from the skillet.
2. Add onion to remaining oil in skillet and cook until tender but not browned. Add tomatoes and chili sauce. Bring to a boil, stirring to scrape up brown bits from the bottom of skillet.
3. Pour sauce over chicken. Cover and bake at 350 F. for 30 to 45 minutes, until chicken is fork tender. Serve with rice or noodles.

1 chicken, cut up
8 tbsp. unseasoned bread crumbs
½ tsp. celery salt
½ tsp. onion powder
Garlic salt
Cayenne or chili powder
Coarse black pepper

Preheat oven to 475 F.
1. Keep chicken well chilled. Trim excess fat and discard. Rinse in ice water. Spray cookie sheet with non-stick cooking spray.
2. Combine crumbs and seasoning in large brown paper bag. Add moist chicken and shake. Put on cookie sheet, skin side up.
3. Bake at 475 F. for 30-45 minutes. Do not turn.

Eat Your Heart Out, Honey!

SOUTHERN STYLE OVEN FRIED CHICKEN

"PARTS 'N PIECES"

Baked

Serves 4

**Cooking Time:
45 Minutes**

MY CHICKEN SCRATCHES:

UP & AT 'EM CHICKEN

"PARTS 'N PIECES"

Baked

Serves 8

Preparation Time:
1 Hour
Cooking Time:
1 Hour

MY CHICKEN SCRATCHES:

_____

_____

_____

_____

1 chicken, cut up
1 ½ cups orange juice
½ cup water
1 cup raw rice
1 onion, chopped
1 red bell pepper, minced
1 clove garlic, minced
½ cup tequila
1 ½ tsp. cumin seeds
¾ tsp. dried oregano
1 medium zucchini, thick slices
1 orange, peeled, sliced

Preheat oven to 350 F.

1. Marinate chicken in orange juice and water for 1 hour or more in the refrigerator. Drain and reserve marinade.
2. Broil chicken, skin side up, just until skin is crisp and well rendered of fat.
3. Combine rice, onion, bell pepper and garlic in the bottom of a non-stick pan. Arrange chicken skin side up on top of the rice mixture.
4. Pour remaining marinade and tequila over chicken and sprinkle with cumin and oregano. Cover and bake 350 F. for 30 minutes. Add zucchini slices. Cover and bake an additional 10 - 12 minutes. Garnish with fresh orange slices.

¾ cup vegetable oil
⅓ cup light corn syrup
½ cup chopped onion
3 tbsp. lemon juice
2 tsp. dried oregano
2 tsp. caraway seed
¼ tsp. salt
2 chickens, split

"" *Chicken Delight* ""

BARBECUED CHICKEN HALVES

"WHOLE"

Broiled or Bar-B-Que

Serves 4

**Preparation Time:
1 Hour
Cooking Time:
50 Minutes**

MY CHICKEN SCRATCHES:

_____

_____

_____

_____

_____

_____

1. Combine oil, syrup, onion, lemon juice, oregano, caraway seed and salt. Marinate chicken in mixture for at least 1 hour.
2. Barbecue for 30 minutes over slow coals. Baste with marinade and turn over and barbecue 15 - 20 minutes longer.
3. Chicken may be broiled instead of barbecued. Place 4 to 5 inches from heat and broil 15 minutes on each side or until tender.

CAMPER CHICKEN

"BREASTS & LEGS"

Broiled or Bar-B-Que

Serves 4 - 5

Preparation Time:
3 Hours
Cooking Time:
20 Minutes

MY CHICKEN SCRATCHES:

_____

_____

_____

_____

_____

3 chicken breasts
6 drumsticks
¾ cup soy sauce
1 clove garlic, crushed
3 tbsp. sugar
3 tbsp. gin

When the going gets tough, the tough go camping

1. Remove skin from chicken. Place chicken in plastic bag and add other ingredients. Seal bag and marinate for 2 - 3 hours.
2. Broil over coals for 20 minutes or until tender, turning several times.

1 envelope Italian salad dressing mix
½ tsp. pepper
⅓ cup grapefruit juice
⅓ cup salad oil
1 chicken, cut up

1. Blend salad dressing mix, pepper, grapefruit juice and salad oil. Pour over chicken pieces. Cover.
2. Chill 6 hours or more.
3. Broil, basting with marinade, 30 - 35 minutes or until tender.

Many men run after a ""chick"" only to find it was a wild goose chase.

Broiled or Bar-B-Que

Serves 4

**Preparation Time:
6 Hours
Cooking Time:
35 Minutes**

MY CHICKEN SCRATCHES:

HOO-HA CHICKEN

"PARTS 'N PIECES"

Broiled or Bar-B-Que

Serves 4

Preparation Time:
12 Hours
Cooking Time:
30 Minutes

MY CHICKEN SCRATCHES:

_____

_____

_____

_____

_____

1 chicken, cut up
1 cup Rose's lime juice
¾ tsp. grated lime rind
1 cup dry vermouth
3 cloves garlic, crushed
¼ tsp. salt
½ tsp. pepper

1. Combine lime juice, lime rind, vermouth, garlic, salt and pepper for the marinade. Marinate chicken in it for several hours or overnight, turning often.
2. Grill over charcoal for 20 minutes or until tender or oven-fry by placing chicken in shallow baking dish lined with foil and bake 350 F. for 35 minutes or until tender. Baste several times while chicken is baking, or barbecuing.

Madam Cluck says...
You may not get what you want,
but you better want what you get

3 chicken breasts, split and skinned
¼ cup orange juice
2 tsp. orange peel, grated
2 tbsp. soy sauce
½ tsp. cinnamon
½ tsp. ginger
½ tsp. curry powder
¼ tsp. pepper

1. Wash and dry chicken breasts; place in baking dish.
2. Combine remaining ingredients and pour over chicken. Cover and refrigerate about 2 hours. Drain and reserve marinade.
3. Broil chicken until crisp and brown and turn to brown the other side.
4. Heat marinade to serve over chicken or hot cooked rice.

Dieters Motto ...
    If at first you don"t recede
      diet again...

LOW CALORIE ORANGE BROILED CHICKEN

"BREASTS"

Broiled or Bar-B-Que

Serves 3 - 5

Preparation Time:
2 Hours
Cooking Time:
30 Minutes

MY CHICKEN SCRATCHES:

_____
_____
_____
_____
_____

MARINATED CHICKEN

"PARTS 'N PIECES"

Broiled or Bar-B-Que

Serves 6 - 8

**Preparation Time:
12 Hours
Cooking Time:
1 Hour**

MY CHICKEN SCRATCHES:

_____

_____

_____

_____

2 chickens, cut up
1 cup dry sherry
¼ cup salad oil
3 tbsp. parsley flakes
1 ½ tsp. salt
1 tbsp. paprika
1 ½ tsp. thyme leaves
1 ½ tsp. basil leaves
1 tsp. tarragon leaves
½ tsp. curry powder
½ tsp. garlic powder
¼ tsp. pepper

Fowl is a 4 letter bird.

1. Place chicken in a tight-fitting container or plastic bag; set aside.
2. Combine remaining ingredients; pour over chicken. Cover and refrigerate 12 hours or longer.
3. Remove chicken from marinade and place on grill over hot charcoal.
4. Broil 45 - 60 minutes, turning and basting often.
5. This recipe can be baked 350 F. for 1 hour or until tender.

1 chicken, split in half or quarters
½ tsp. salt
¼ cup butter, melted
¼ cup apple or berry jelly
⅓ cup white table wine

1. Sprinkle chicken with salt. Brush generously with butter, place on broiler pan, skin side down. Place broiler about 8" from the heat.
2. Combine remaining butter with jelly and wine and heat until jelly melts.
3. After chicken has cooked 15 minutes, baste with jelly-wine mixture. Turn and continue cooking, basting and turning frequently until well browned and tender, broiling about 40 minutes.

NORMANDY CHICKEN

"WHOLE"

Broiled or Bar-B-Que

Serves 4

**Cooking Time:
40 Minutes**

MY CHICKEN SCRATCHES:

_____

_____

_____

_____

_____

SUNRISE CHICKEN

"BREASTS"

Broiled or Bar-B-Que

Serves 4

Preparation Time:
1 Hour
Cooking Time:
15 Minutes

MY CHICKEN SCRATCHES:

_____
_____
_____
_____
_____

3 chicken breasts, split, skinned and boned
½ cup olive oil
¼ cup honey
¼ cup soy sauce
3 tbsp. dry sherry
3 tbsp. onion, grated
1 large garlic clove, crushed
½ tsp. pepper
2 tbsp. sesame seeds, toasted

1. Cut the chicken breast halves crosswise into four equal-sized pieces. In a large bowl, combine the oil, honey, soy sauce, sherry, onion, garlic and pepper.
2. Add the chicken pieces and turn to coat them well. Cover and refrigerate overnight. When ready to cook, preheat the broiler. Thread six pieces of the chicken on each of four 10" wooden skewers and broil five or six inches from the heat for about five minutes per side.
3. Heat the marinade in a saucepan. Brush the cooked sates with the hot marinade and sprinkle with the toasted sesame seeds.

Going
Undercover
(CASSEROLE)

2 pkg. frozen artichoke hearts,
   thawed (10 oz. ea.)
3 chicken breasts, halved and boned
Pepper
¼ lb. bacon, cooked and crumbed
1 cup grated Cheddar cheese
3 tbsp. grated Parmesan cheese
1 ½ cups dry vermouth

Preheat oven to 350 F.
1. Arrange artichoke hearts in a casserole. Top with chicken and season with pepper to taste. Sprinkle with bacon and cheeses. Add vermouth.
2. Bake uncovered at 350 F. for 1 ½ hours. Add more vermouth, if necessary to keep moist.

Casseroles

Serves 4

**Cooking Time:
1 ½ Hour**

MY CHICKEN SCRATCHES:

_____

_____

_____

_____

_____

CHICKEN A L'ORANGE

"PARTS 'N PIECES"

Casseroles

Serves 4

Cooking Time:
1 Hour

MY CHICKEN SCRATCHES:

_____

_____

_____

_____

½ tsp. ginger
1 tsp. salt
Pepper to taste
½ cup cornflakes, crushed
1 chicken, cut up
2 tbsp. oil
2 tsp. cornstarch
1 cup orange juice
1 tbsp. grated peel
Fresh chopped parsley

Preheat oven to 350 F.

1. Mix ginger, salt, pepper and cornflakes. Use to coat chicken.
2. Brown chicken in 1" hot oil. Remove chicken and place in baking dish.
3. Keep 2 tbsp. drippings. Stir in cornstarch, orange juice and grated orange peel. Cook until thick.
4. Pour over chicken. Sprinkle with parsley.
5. Cover and bake 350 F. for 1 hour or until tender.

1 chicken, cut in half
2 large carrots, cut in 1" pieces
2 medium potatoes, quartered
1 cup frozen peas, unthawed
½ tsp. salt
¼ tsp. pepper
½ tsp. thyme leaves
2 tbsp. butter

""*Tricks of the Trade*""

Preheat oven to 375 F.
1. Tear 2 pieces of heavy duty foil, 16" x 18". Arrange chicken and vegetables sprinkled with seasonings. Dot with butter. Seal foil with double foil wrap on top and sides.
2. Place bundles in shallow pan and bake 375 F. for 1 hour. To cook, if frozen, bake 375 F. for 1 ½ hours.

Make ahead and freeze — ready for a no-time-to-cook meal.

CHICKEN IN SILVER BUNDLES

"WHOLE"

Casseroles

Serves 4

**Cooking Time:
1 Hour**

MY CHICKEN SCRATCHES:

_____

_____

_____

_____

_____

CHICKEN MARENGO

"BREASTS"

Casseroles

Serves 4

Cooking Time:
1 Hour 20 Minutes

MY CHICKEN SCRATCHES:

_____

_____

_____

_____

4 chicken breasts, skinned and boned
½ tsp. salt
½ tsp. pepper
1 cup boiling water
1 pkg. instant chicken broth and seasoning mix or
   1 chicken bouillon
2 tbsp. dehydrated onion flakes
1 tsp. sherry extract
1 garlic clove, minced
¼ tsp. marjoram leaves
2 medium cans tomatoes, drained
½ cup sliced mushrooms, canned or fresh

Preheat oven to 325 F.
1. Sprinkle chicken with salt and pepper. Brown on all sides over moderate heat in a non-stick skillet. Place chicken in a baking dish.
2. Combine water and broth mix. Let stand 5 minutes. Add onion flakes, sherry extract, garlic and marjoram to broth mixture.
3. Spoon half of sauce over chicken. Bake 325 F. for 20 minutes.
4. Spoon remaining sauce over chicken and bake 15 minutes longer or until chicken is tender.
5. Heat tomatoes and mushrooms in a saucepan. Spoon over chicken.

¾ cup flour
½ tsp. salt
1 tsp. pepper
1 chicken, cut up
¼ cup olive oil
1 cup fresh mushrooms, sliced
½ cup onion, sliced

½ clove garlic, pressed
½ tsp. tarragon leaves
¼ cup Rhine wine
¼ cup chicken broth
½ lemon, juiced
1 tbsp. flour
Hot cooked rice

CHICKEN TARRAGON

"PARTS 'N PIECES"

Casseroles

Serves 4

Cooking Time:
1 Hour 15 Minutes

Preheat oven to 350 F.

1. Put flour, salt and pepper in a paper bag. Place chicken pieces in bag and shake to coat chicken. Brown coated chicken in olive oil in flame-proof casserole. Remove chicken from casserole.
2. Lightly saute mushrooms, onion and garlic in pan drippings. Add tarragon, wine, chicken broth and lemon juice to casserole. Heat over low heat.
3. Return chicken to casserole, spooning sauce over chicken. Cover and bake 350 F. for 45 minutes or until chicken is tender. Remove chicken to warm platter.
4. Mix sauce with flour until smooth, stir into drippings. Cook, stirring, over medium heat, until thickened. Serve with chicken and gravy over hot cooked rice.

MY CHICKEN SCRATCHES:

GREEN AND GOLD CHICKEN

"BREASTS 'N THIGHS"

Casseroles

Serves 6 - 8

**Cooking Time:
1 ¼ Hours**

MY CHICKEN SCRATCHES:

_____

_____

_____

_____

_____

3 chicken breasts
6 chicken thighs
Onion salt to taste
Celery salt to taste
2 pkgs. broccoli, thawed
Sliced mushrooms (optional)
2 cans cream of chicken soup (10 ½ oz. ea.)
¼ tsp. curry powder
1 lemon, juiced
4 tbsp. sherry
1 cup Cheddar cheese, grated

Worth a standing ovation

Preheat oven to 350 F.
1. Lay chicken parts in greased baking dish. Season with onion salt and celery salt. Cover with foil. Bake 350 F. for 1 hour. Reserve juice from chicken.
2. Arrange baked chicken and broccoli in 9"x 13" baking dish with mushrooms.
3. Combine and blend soup, curry, juice from lemon and sherry. Add juice from baked chicken until desired thickness.
4. Pour over chicken, cover with cheese and bake, uncovered, at 325 F. until bubbly.

½ cup milk
½ tsp. salt
1 can cream of mushroom soup (10 ½ oz.)
1 can chop suey vegetables (14 oz.)
2 pkgs. frozen french style green beans,
    thawed (9 oz.)
3 cups chicken, cooked and diced
⅓ cup onion, chopped
1 ½ cups Cheddar cheese, cubed or grated
1 can french fried onions, (3 ½ oz.)

Preheat oven to 350 F.
1. Stir milk and salt into soup until smooth.
2. Drain chop suey vegetables. Fold into soup, along with green beans, chicken and onion, add cheese.
3. Spoon mix into 8" x 12" baking dish. Bake 350 F. for 45 minutes or until beans are tender.
4. Remove from oven and top with french fried onions and return to oven for about 10 minutes. Allow to stand 10 minutes before serving.

GREEN BEAN CASEROLE

"PARTS 'N PIECES"

Casseroles

Serves 6 - 8

**Cooking Time:
55 Minutes**

MY CHICKEN SCRATCHES:

_____

_____

_____

_____

_____

HERBED CHICKEN EN CASSEROLE

"BREASTS"

Casseroles

Serves 3 - 5

Cooking Time:
1 Hour

MY CHICKEN SCRATCHES:

_____

_____

_____

_____

_____

3 large chicken breasts, split
Salt and pepper to taste
¼ cup margarine or butter
1 can condensed cream of chicken soup (10 ½ oz.)
¾ cup cooking sauterne wine
1 can water chestnuts, drained and sliced (5 oz.)
1 can broiled sliced mushrooms, drained (3 oz.)
3 tbsp. green pepper, chopped
¼ tsp. crushed thyme

Preheat oven to 350 F.
1. Lightly season chicken with salt and pepper. Brown slowly in butter in skillet.
2. Arrange browned chicken, skin-side up in baking dish.
3. To make the sauce, add soup to drippings in skillet. Slowly add sauterne, stirring until smooth. Add remaining ingredients and heat to boiling. Pour sauce over chicken.
4. Cover with foil and bake in 350 F. oven for 25 minutes. Uncover and continue baking 25 - 30 minutes longer, or until chicken is tender. Serve with hot fluffy rice or buttered noodles.

3 tbsp. butter
1 small clove garlic, sliced
2 medium onions, sliced
1 medium eggplant, sliced
1 chicken, cut up
1 envelope seasoned coating mix

I'm game if you are

Preheat oven to 350 F.
1. Melt butter in 9" x 13" baking dish. Stir in garlic and onions.
2. Add vegetables and stir to coat with butter.
3. Bake 350 F. for 10 minutes.
4. Coat chicken pieces with coating mix and sprinkle any remaining mix over vegetables. Top with chicken pieces and bake 50 minutes longer.

RATATOUILLE

"PARTS 'N PIECES"

Casseroles

Serves 4

**Cooking Time:
1 Hour**

MY CHICKEN SCRATCHES:

_____

_____

_____

_____

_____

RICE 'N EASY

"BREASTS"

Casseroles

Serves 4

**Cooking Time:
1 Hour**

MY CHICKEN SCRATCHES:

_____

_____

_____

_____

_____

⅓ cup dry white wine
¾ cup chicken broth or water
½ tsp. salt
1 ½ cups instant rice, raw
4 chicken breasts, split
1 can sliced mushrooms, undrained (6 oz.)
1 can cream of mushroom soup (10 ½ oz.)
½ tsp. thyme leaves
1 tbsp. bread crumbs
3 tsp. butter, melted

Preheat oven to 400 F.
1. In 7" x 11" greased baking dish, combine wine, chicken broth or water, salt and rice.
2. Place chicken breasts over rice mixture. Combine mushrooms, undrained with mushroom soup. Spread over chicken.
3. Sprinkle with thyme leaves, bread crumbs and melted butter. Cover lightly with foil and bake 400 F. for 1 hour or until chicken is tender.

Foreign A'Faire
(CONTINENTAL)

Oil
1 cup rice
1 onion, sliced
Water
1 can consomme (10 ½ oz.)
½ cup currants
1 chicken, cut-up
½ cup flour
1 tsp. salt
¼ tsp. pepper
1 tsp. cinnamon
1 - 2 tbsp. oil

ARMENIAN CINNAMON CHICKEN

"PARTS 'N PIECES"

Continental

Serves 4

**Cooking Time:
1 ½ Hour**

Preheat oven to 350 F.

1. Heat 1 tbsp. oil in skillet, add rice and onion and cook until lightly browned. Put rice in 9x13" pan. Add consomme (plus water to equal 2 cups) and currants. Stir to mix.

2. Remove fat from chicken and at least half of the loose skin. Combine flour, salt, pepper and cinnamon. Dredge chicken in the flour mixture.

3. Heat 1-2 tbsp. oil in skillet. Add chicken and brown. Place chicken on top of rice. Cover and bake 350 F. for 1 hour. Uncover and bake ½ hour longer.

MY CHICKEN SCRATCHES:

"BLUE EYES"
ITALIAN CHICKEN

"PARTS 'N PIECES"

Continental

Serves 8

**Cooking Time:
1 ½ Hours**

MY CHICKEN SCRATCHES:

_____

_____

_____

_____

_____

2 chickens, cut-up
Olive oil
2 white onions, thinly sliced
8 large potatoes (cut in quarters)
Salt and pepper, to taste
3 tbsp. oregano
1 cup parsley, chopped

"" Cooking It, My Way ""

Preheat oven to 350 F.

1. Soak chicken covered with salted water, for about ½ hour. Fill 9x13" baking dish with about 1 inch of olive oil. Pat chicken dry, place in dish.
2. Place onion slices on chicken. Add potatoes, pepper, salt, oregano and parsley. Toss everything by hand until well mixed.
3. Place in 350 F. oven to about 1 - 1 ½ hours, stirring every 10 - 15 minutes. Let dish remain in oven until potatoes are soft.

4 strips bacon, diced
1 onion, chopped
1 carrot, diced
1 chicken, cut-up
¼ cup brandy
2 tbsp. flour
1 ½ cup burgundy
½ cup chicken broth

2 tbsp. tomato paste
½ tsp. salt
2 garlic cloves, chopped
1 small bay leaf
¼ tsp. thyme
¼ tsp. ground pepper
6 sprigs parsley

CHICKEN FRANCOIS

"PARTS 'N PIECES"

Continental

Serves 4 - 6

Cooking Time: 1 Hour

MY CHICKEN SCRATCHES:

_____

_____

_____

_____

_____

1. Cook bacon, onion and carrot in large skillet over moderate heat until bacon is crisp and vegetables lightly brown. Scoop out bacon and vegetables and set aside.
2. Brown chicken slowly. Pour brandy over browned chicken and ignite. When flame dies out, stir flour into fat in pan.
3. Add burgundy, broth and tomato paste, stirring to blend with flour mixture. Return vegetables and bacon to skillet. Add salt, garlic, bay leaf, thyme and pepper. Lay parsley on top.
4. Heat to boiling, cover and turn heat low. Simmer 30 minutes or until chicken is tender. Remove parsley before serving.

Oooh, La La!

MY CHICKEN SCRATCHES:

_____

_____

_____

_____

_____

1 small onion, chopped
1 tbsp. oil
★ 3 cans chili salsa (7 oz.)
1 pkg. corn chips, slightly crushed (1 lb.)
1 chicken, cooked and diced
1 ¾ lb. Velveeta cheese
7 tbsp. canned evaporated milk or chicken broth

Preheat oven to 350 F.
1. Saute chopped onion in oil. Add salsa and simmer for 10 minutes.
2. Using a 9x13" glass dish, start with a layer of chips, then a layer of chicken, a layer of cheese and a layer of sauce. Repeat layers, saving chips for the top. Spoon canned milk or broth over the top and bake at 350 F. for 45 minutes.

★ **NOTE:** If you like less pepper, use 2 cans Tomato & Green Chile Salsa and 4 oz. (½ cup) tomato juice.

1 egg white, beaten
1 tsp. cornstarch
2 tsp. water
3 chicken breasts, boned and diced
½ cup oil
¼ tsp. garlic, minced
¼ tsp. ginger
2 tsp. onion, grated
6 tsp. soy sauce
2 tsp. sugar
1 tsp. sesame oil
½ tsp. wine
½ tsp. pepper
2 tsp. cornstarch

Confucius Say . . .
Wicked chickens
lay deviled eggs!

1. Combine egg white, 1 tsp. cornstarch and water and marinate chicken for 30 minutes. Fry chicken until golden brown, leaving 4 tbsp. oil in the skillet.
2. Stir fry garlic, ginger and onion. Add chicken, stir fry.
3. In saucepan, combine soy sauce, sugar, sesame oil, wine, pepper and 2 tsp. cornstarch. Cook until sauce thickens. Pour sauce over chicken.

CONFUCIUS CHICKEN

"BREASTS"

Continental

Serves 4 - 6

**Preparation Time:
30 Minutes
Cooking Time:
45 Minutes**

MY CHICKEN SCRATCHES:

_____
_____
_____
_____
_____

COQ AU VIN CHICKEN

"BREASTS"

Continental

Serves 4

Cooking Time: 1 Hour

MY CHICKEN SCRATCHES:

_____

_____

_____

_____

4 chicken breasts, split and skinned
½ tsp. salt
½ tsp. pepper
2 cups chicken bouillon
1 cup mushrooms, sliced
2 stalks celery, sliced
3 tbsp. dehydrated onion flakes
2 sprigs parsley
1 bay leaf
1 tsp. sherry extract
1 can tomatoes, chopped (16 oz.)

*It Ain"t the Men in Your Life.
It's the Life in Your Men*

Preheat oven to 350 F.

1. Sprinkle chicken with salt and pepper. Brown chicken in non-stick pan over high heat, turning frequently. Transfer to baking dish. Bake 350 F. for 35 minutes.
2. Meanwhile, combine bouillon, mushrooms, celery, onion flakes, parsley and bay leaf in saucepan. Simmer 30 minutes. Add sherry extract and tomatoes. Pour over chicken.

1 chicken, cut-up
1 can tomatoes, undrained (16 oz.)
1 onion, chopped
1 green pepper, chopped
1 cup celery, sliced
1 can mushrooms, undrained (4 oz.)
2 tbsp. dried parsley
1 tsp. oregano
1 tbsp. Worcestershire sauce

CREOLE CHICKEN

"PARTS 'N PIECES"

Continental

Serves 4

**Cooking Time:
1 Hour**

1. Spray non-stick coating in electric skillet. Arrange chicken, skin side down. Add 1 tbsp. water. Turn heat to moderate. When water evaporates, chicken will brown in its own fat.
2. Turn to brown evenly. Drain. Turn chicken skin side up.
3. Add remaining ingredients, cover tightly and simmer until tender and sauce is thick, about 50-60 minutes.

Serve over rice!

MY CHICKEN SCRATCHES:

_____

_____

_____

_____

_____

MAUI CHICKEN

"WHOLE"

Continental

Serves 5 - 6

Cooking Time:
2 Hours

MY CHICKEN SCRATCHES:

_____

_____

_____

_____

1 chicken, whole
½ cup celery, chopped
2 tbsp. onion, chopped
3 tbsp. butter
¼ cup syrup from pineapple
1 tbsp. lemon juice
2 cups pkg. cornbread
  stuffing mix

¼ cup shredded coconut
2 tsp. flour
½ tsp. paprika
1 cup water
1 can crushed pineapple,
  drained (8 ¼ oz.)

Preheat oven to 400 F.

1. Sprinkle body cavity with salt. Saute celery and onion lightly in 2 tbsp. butter. Add ¼ cup pineapple syrup, lemon juice and heat to boiling. Pour over stuffing mix, tossing to moisten evenly. Add pineapple and coconut and mix well.

2. Stuff lightly into body and neck of the chicken and skewer openings. Tie legs together, close to the body and tie wings close to breast. Place in roasting pan.

3. Melt remaining tbsp. butter and mix with flour and paprika. Brush over skin.

4. Bake 400 F. for 30 minutes or until skin begins to brown. Pour water into baking pan and cover, using foil if pan does not have a lid.

5. Reset oven to 325 F. and bake 1 ½ hours longer until chicken is very tender. Remove strings and skewers before serving.

3 chicken breasts, split
1 can juice-packed pear halves (16 oz.)
2 tbsp. lemon juice
2 tbsp. soy sauce
1 ¼ tsp. Oriental 5-spice powder
   (or pumpkin pie spice)
Paprika

Preheat oven to 400 F.

1. Arrange chicken breast halves, skin-side up in a shallow baking pan. Bake uncovered 400 F. for 20 minutes, until skin is crisp. Drain and discard fat.
2. Drain pears and reserve juice. Pour pear juice, lemon juice and soy sauce over chicken. Sprinkle with 5-spice powder. Bake uncovered 25 minutes, basting often.
3. Slice pear halves into quarters and arrange around chicken. Baste with pan juices and bake 5 - 6 minutes more, until heated through. Sprinkle lightly with paprika.

SPICY ORIENTAL CHICKEN & PEARS

"BREASTS"

Continental

Serves 4 - 6

**Cooking Time:
25 Minutes**

MY CHICKEN SCRATCHES:

_____

_____

_____

_____

_____

YOGURT CHICKEN

"PARTS 'N PIECES"

Continental

Serves 4

Preparation Time:
24 Hours
Cooking Time:
1 Hour

MY CHICKEN SCRATCHES:

_____

_____

_____

_____

_____

1 chicken, cut up
¼ cup lemon juice
1 carton Yogurt
1 tsp. cumin seeds
2 - 3 bay leaves
2 tsp. dried mint leaves, crushed
¼ cup oil
1 tsp. ginger powder
   (or 1 tsp. fresh grated)

2 tsp. garlic powder
2 tsp. onion powder
1 tsp. salt
1 tsp. black pepper
1 tsp. cayenne pepper
   (or paprika - less hot)

Preheat oven to 350 F.

1. Marinate chicken with the lemon juice for about 30 minutes. Mix yogurt and all the remaining ingredients in a separate bowl and pour over chicken. Mix well.
2. Let this set at room temperature, preferably overnight, or at least 4 - 5 hours. After this time, the chicken may be placed in the refrigerator until cooking time.
3. Place in shallow 8x12" baking dish. Cover with yogurt mixture and bake at 350 F. for 45 - 60 minutes. Serve with rice pilaf.

The longer you marinate, the more tender the chicken.

JUST YOU AND ME, BABE
(For One Or Two)

2 chicken breasts, split
¾ tsp. seasoned salt
2 tbsp. oil
½ cup cheese cracker crumbs, crushed

Preheat oven to 375 F.
1. Sprinkle chicken breasts with seasoned salt.
2. Brush with oil and roll in cracker crumbs.
3. Place on flat baking sheet.
4. Bake 375 F. for 1 hour or until brown and tender.

Chicken Coquette is a
""Flirtatious Hen""

CHEESE-Y CHICKEN

"BREASTS"

For One or Two

Serves 2

Cooking Time:
1 Hour

MY CHICKEN SCRATCHES:

_____

_____

_____

_____

_____

CHICKEN AND ARTICHOKE HEARTS

"BREASTS"

For One or Two

Serves 2

Cooking Time: 30 Minutes

MY CHICKEN SCRATCHES:

_____
_____
_____
_____
_____

¼ cup vegetable oil
1 clove garlic, crushed
½ lemon with rind, cut into thin slices
½ lb. fresh mushrooms, sliced
2 chicken breasts, skinned, boned & diced
1 tbsp. flour
¼ cup dry white wine
½ tsp. salt
½ tsp. pepper
½ tsp. oregano
1 can whole artichoke hearts (unmarinated) (14 oz.)

1. Heat oil in frying pan over medium heat. Add garlic and saute until soft. Add lemon and mushrooms and saute until soft.
2. Stir in all other ingredients except the artichokes. Fry, stirring frequently, approximately 15 minutes or until chicken is tender.
3. Add the artichokes and heat through.

Note: The cooked lemon rind does remain as part of the served preparation. It adds an unusual taste and texture.

2 chicken breasts, skinned and boned
¼ tsp. salt
½ tsp. tarragon
½ tsp. pepper
1 cup chicken bouillon
½ tsp. sherry extract
2 tbsp. dehydrated onion flakes
½ cup sliced mushrooms
4 oz. snow peas, fresh or frozen
¼ cup scallions to garnish

Be Daring. "Dahling"

1. Cut chicken into 2 x 1" strips. Sprinkle with salt, tarragon and pepper.
2. Combine chicken bouillon and sherry extract in skillet. Bring to a simmer over low heat. Add chicken strips and onion flakes. Cook 10 minutes or until strips are white and tender.
3. Add mushrooms and snow peas. Cook just until vegetables are heated through, but snow peas are still crisp. Serve garnished with scallions.

Note: Fresh or frozen peas may be used instead of snow peas.

CHICKEN AND SNOW PEAS

"BREASTS"

For One or Two

Serves 2

Cooking Time: 15 Minutes

MY CHICKEN SCRATCHES:

_____

_____

_____

_____

_____

CHICKEN FOR ONE

"LEG 'N THIGH"

For One or Two

Serves 1

**Cooking Time:
40 Minutes**

MY CHICKEN SCRATCHES:

_____

_____

_____

_____

_____

**2 tbsp. butter, melted
1 tsp. brandy
¼ tsp. garlic powder
⅛ tsp. cayenne pepper
1 chicken leg and thigh
¼ tsp. seasoning salt**

1. In baking dish, mix butter, brandy, garlic powder and cayenne. Add chicken skin side up in baking dish.
2. Broil 8" from the heat for 20 minutes. Turn and brush with remaining butter mixture and sprinkle remaining seasoning salt.
3. Broil 15 minutes longer or until tender.

*Two can live as cheaply as one,
if one doesn"t eat*

1 chicken breast, split, skinned and boned
2 thin slices mozzarella cheese
3 tbsp. minced onion
2 tbsp. minced fresh parsley
1 can tomato sauce (8 oz.)
1 can mushrooms (4 oz.)
2 tbsp. white wine or water
Dried garlic
Oregano
Basil

Preheat oven to 350 F.
1. Top each piece of chicken with a slice of cheese and a sprinkle of onion and parsley.
2. Roll up and place skin side down in small baking dish.
3. Combine remaining ingredients and spoon over chicken rolls. Bake uncovered 350 F. for 35 minutes, basting several times.

Tempting
Tempting

CHICKEN PARMIGIANA ROLLS

"BREASTS"

For One or Two

Serves 1

Cooking Time: 35 Minutes

MY CHICKEN SCRATCHES:

_____

_____

_____

_____

_____

71

CHINESE CHICKEN NOODLE PANCAKE

"PARTS 'N PIECES"

For One or Two

Serves 2

Cooking Time:
20 Minutes

MY CHICKEN SCRATCHES:

_____

_____

_____

_____

_____

1 chicken bouillon cube
⅔ cup boiling water
2 tbsp. oil
2 cups thin noodles, cooked and drained
2 tbsp. sherry wine or water
2 tbsp. cornstarch
½ to ¾ lb. raw chicken, cut in strips
1 pkg. Chinese style stir fry vegetables (10 oz.)

1. Dissolve bouillon cube in water and set aside. Heat 2 tbsp. oil in skillet. Spread noodles evenly in skillet and brown lightly without stirring. Turn in one piece and brown other side. Place on platter and keep warm (do not cover).
2. Combine sherry and cornstarch, pour over chicken and mix to coat evenly. Add remaining oil to skillet.
3. Add chicken and saute until lightly browned. Move to one side of pan.
4. Prepare vegetables in pan as directed on package. Substitute the bouillon for the water. Serve chicken mixture over pancake.

½ cup sour cream
2 tsp. lemon juice
1 tbsp. milk
½ tsp. salt
½ tsp. rosemary, crumbled
½ tsp. paprika
⅛ tsp. pepper
1 chicken, split in half or quarters
1 ½ tbsp. cornflake crumbs

Preheat oven to 375 F.
1. Blend sour cream, lemon juice, milk, salt, rosemary, paprika and pepper.
2. Arrange chicken, skin side up, in 9x13" baking dish. Brush generously with sour cream mixture using about ⅓ cup.
3. Bake 375 F. for 50 minutes. Remove from oven and brush with remaining sour cream mixture. Sprinkle with cornflake crumbs. Return to oven for 10 minutes.

CRISP 'N CREAMY BAKE

"WHOLE"

For One or Two

Serves 2 or 3

**Cooking Time:
1 Hour**

MY CHICKEN SCRATCHES:

_____
_____
_____
_____
_____

CRUNCHY BAKE

"BREASTS"

For One or Two

Serves 1

**Cooking Time:
45 Minutes**

MY CHICKEN SCRATCHES:

_____

_____

_____

_____

1 envelope cream of chicken soup
⅓ cup hot water
1 chicken breast, split
¾ cup herb seasoned stuffing mix, crushed
2 tbsp. butter, melted

Preheat oven to 375 F.
1. In bowl, blend soup mix and water. Dip chicken in soup then in crumbs.
2. Place in shallow baking dish and drizzle with butter.
3. Bake 375 F. for 45 minutes or until tender.

Keeping a ""breast of the situation""

2 chicken breasts, split, skinned and boned
½ tsp. salt
½ tsp. pepper
⅛ tsp. thyme, crushed
2 tbsp. butter
2 tbsp. white wine
1 kiwifruit, pared and sliced

1. Pound chicken between pieces of plastic wrap to flatten to ¼ inch. Sprinkle with salt, pepper and thyme.
2. Heat butter in skillet. Saute chicken on medium-high heat about 4 minutes or until cooked and tender. Turn once half-way through cooking time. Remove to platter and keep warm.
3. Add wine to skillet. Cook and stir 2 minutes. Add kiwifruit. Cook and stir gently 30 seconds longer.

Making Time

QUICK CHICKEN SAUTE

"BREASTS"

For One or Two

Serves 2

Cooking Time: 10 Minutes

MY CHICKEN SCRATCHES:

_____
_____
_____
_____
_____
_____

SPICY DRUMSTICK BAKE

"LEGS"

For One or Two

Serves 2

Cooking Time:
30 minutes

MY CHICKEN SCRATCHES:

_____

_____

_____

_____

_____

4 chicken drumsticks
2 tbsp. mayonnaise
1 cup corn chips, crushed
1 ½ tsp. chili powder
¼ tsp. salt

Preheat oven to 400 F.
1. Brush drumsticks with mayonnaise. Combine corn chips, chili powder and salt. Mix well.
2. Roll drumsticks in mixture and arrange in greased shallow baking dish.
3. Bake 400 F. for 30 minutes or until chicken is browned and tender.

They let the chicken join the band because he was the only one with the drumsticks...

Way To
A Man's
Heart

(FRIED)

1 chicken, cut up
½ tsp. salt
¼ tsp. pepper
3 onions, sliced
½ cup water

1. Place chicken, skin side down, in single layer in large frying pan. Sprinkle with salt and pepper. Place onion slices on top. Cover tightly.
2. Cook over low heat for 30 minutes. Vent lid so liquid will evaporate. Continue cooking for 30 minutes longer or until tender.
3. Place chicken on serving dish leaving onions in pan. Add water and mix with pan drippings. Cook onions until liquid evaporates. Spoon over chicken.

CHICKEN FRIED with ONIONS

"PARTS 'N PIECES"

Fried

Serves 4

**Cooking Time:
1 ¼ Hours**

MY CHICKEN SCRATCHES

CHICKEN PAPRIKA

"PARTS 'N PIECES"

Fried

Serves 4 - 6

**Cooking Time:
45 Minutes**

MY CHICKEN SCRATCHES:

_____

_____

_____

_____

1 chicken, cut up
¼ cup flour, sifted
3 tbsp. paprika
2 tbsp. butter
2 tbsp. oil
½ envelope dry onion soup mix
¼ tsp. salt
1 cup hot water
½ cup green pepper, chopped
1 cup half and half

1. Roll chicken in flour mixed with 1 tsp. paprika. Shake off and reserve excess flour. Heat butter and oil in the skillet.
2. Add chicken and brown slowly. Drain off excess fat.
3. Stir onion soup mix and salt into hot water. Pour over chicken, heat to boiling and cover. Turn heat low and simmer 25 minutes, adding green pepper last 5 minutes.
4. Remove chicken to serving dish. Stir remaining paprika and 1 tbsp. reserved flour mixture into half and half. Add to liquid in skillet. Simmer 3 minutes, stirring until sauce thickens. Pour over chicken and serve at once.

6 chicken thighs
½ tsp. salt
½ tsp. pepper
½ cup onion, chopped
½ cup celery, chopped
1 clove garlic, minced
1 can tomatoes, (1 lb.)
¾ tsp. mixed Italian herbs
½ cup green pepper strips
Hot cooked spaghetti

I only have "Thighs" for you...

1. Sprinkle chicken with salt and pepper. Place in heated, lightly oiled skillet and brown slowly on both sides.
2. Add onions, celery and garlic and saute a few minutes until onion is transparent. Add tomatoes, breaking them up. Sprinkle with herbs.
3. Bring to a boil, cover and turn heat low. Simmer, covered, 30 minutes. Uncover, add green pepper and simmer, uncovered, for 10-15 minutes until sauce thickens slightly. Serve with hot cooked spaghetti.

CHICKEN THIGHS ROMANO

"THIGHS"

Fried

Serves 3

**Cooking Time:
1 Hour**

MY CHICKEN SCRATCHES:

_____

_____

_____

_____

_____

CRISPY HERB CHICKEN

"PARTS 'N PIECES"

Fried

Serves 4

Cooking Time:
45 Minutes

MY CHICKEN SCRATCHES:

_____

_____

_____

_____

_____

½ cup flour
¼ cup fine dry bread crumbs
¼ tsp. tarragon leaves
¼ tsp. chives
¼ tsp. parsley flakes
⅛ tsp. black pepper
¼ tsp. garlic salt
1 chicken, cut up

Talk of the Town

Preheat large skillet with 1" oil to 400 F.
1. Mix together flour, bread crumbs, tarragon, chives, parsley, pepper and garlic salt. Coat chicken pieces with flour and herb mixture.
2. Fry chicken pieces until golden brown, on one side, about 8 to 10 minutes.
3. Turn pieces and continue frying until evenly browned and tender. Remove chicken from oil and drain.

1 chicken, cut up
Salt and pepper to taste
⅓ cup peanut butter
1 tsp. dried tarragon
1 egg, beaten
1 cup flour
5 tbsp. butter
4 tbsp. olive oil

1. Wash chicken, pat dry and season with salt and pepper. Let sit 10 minutes.
2. Mix peanut butter with tarragon. Smear peanut-butter mixture under the skin of the chicken. Dip chicken in egg and then in seasoned flour.
3. Melt butter with olive oil and add chicken skin side down. Cook 10-15 minutes, then turn and cook on other side until tender.

PEANUT-BUTTER FRIED CHICKEN

"PARTS 'N PIECES"

Fried

Serves 4

**Cooking Time:
45 Minutes**

MY CHICKEN SCRATCHES:

_____
_____
_____
_____
_____
_____

REAL SOUTHERN FRIED CHICKEN

"PARTS 'N PIECES"

Fried

Serves 8 - 10

**Preparation Time:
45 Minutes
Cooking Time:
1 Hour**

MY CHICKEN SCRATCHES:

_____

_____

_____

_____

_____

2 chickens, cut up
2 cups milk or buttermilk
1½ cups flour
½ tsp. salt
1 tsp. pepper
1½ lb. shortening

We ain"t just whistling Dixie

1. In large shallow bowl, soak chicken pieces in milk for about 30 minutes. Shake off excess milk from chicken and shake pieces in bag with flour seasoned with salt and pepper. Lay coated pieces out on the counter and let stand about 15 minutes.
2. In large skillet, melt shortening to the depth of 1 ½". When hot enough to sizzle, add chicken pieces. (Do not crowd or they will not brown evenly.)
3. Cook over medium heat until all pieces are brown on one side. Turn chicken using tongs and brown on other side. Be careful not to let flour burn.
4. When chicken is brown on both sides, reduce heat and cook, turning occasionally until done, about 20-30 minutes. Drain on paper towels.

4 chicken breasts, boned
1 green pepper
1 sweet red pepper
2 tbsp. oil
2 tbsp. butter
¾ tsp. dried rosemary
¼ cup white port wine
¼ tsp. salt
½ tsp. pepper

Great Stir Fry!

1. Cut breasts in strips 2" long and 1" wide. Set aside. Core, seed and cut peppers into lengthwise strips.
2. Place oil and butter in large pan and heat. Add pepper strips and stir fry until crisp cooked.
3. Add chicken and rosemary and stir fry for 3 minutes until chicken has turned white. Add wine, salt and pepper and turn up heat and continue to stir fry until wine has evaporated. Do not overcook. Serve immediately.

Note: Chicken and peppers may be prepared in advance, wrapping well in separate wrappings and refrigerate until hour before cooking.

SAUTEED CHICKEN BREASTS

"BREASTS"

Fried

Serves 4

Cooking Time:
15 Minutes

MY CHICKEN SCRATCHES:

_____

_____

_____

_____

_____

_____

TARRAGON CHICKEN

"BREASTS"

Fried

Serves 6

Cooking Time:
1 Hour

MY CHICKEN SCRATCHES:

_____

_____

_____

_____

_____

½ lb. fresh mushrooms
¼ cup margarine
6 large chicken breasts
1 tbsp. poultry seasoning
¾ tsp. tarragon
1 cup white wine
1 cup sour cream
1 cup green onions, chopped
salt and pepper

For My Hen Parties

1. Slice mushrooms and saute in 2 tbsp. margarine, until golden. Remove mushrooms and reserve. Add the rest of the margarine and brown the chicken well. Sprinkle with the poultry seasoning during browning.
2. Add mushrooms. Sprinkle with tarragon and pour wine over chicken. Cover and simmer for 45 minutes until tender. Season to taste.
3. Spoon sour cream into pan juices after removing chicken. Sprinkle with green onions to serve.

SLIM
CHICK

(Low Calorie)

1 chicken, cut up
½ tsp. salt
¼ tsp. pepper
½ tsp. paprika
2 tbsp. salad oil
Juice of ½ lemon
½ cup water
½ tsp. savory
¼ tsp. thyme
1 clove garlic, minced
1 onion, sliced
1 green pepper, cut in strips
½ lb. mushrooms

Everything comes to she who "weights"

1. Sprinkle chicken with salt, pepper and paprika. Heat oil in skillet. Place chicken skin side down in hot oil. Brown well on both sides.
2. Add lemon juice, water, herbs and garlic. Cover and cook, 20 minutes. Add vegetables and cook 10 minutes longer or until chicken is tender.

CHICKEN A LA' VEGETABLES

"PARTS 'N PIECES"

Low Calorie

Serves 4

Cooking Time: 1 Hour

MY CHICKEN SCRATCHES:

_____
_____
_____
_____
_____

CHICKEN BREASTS in ORANGE SAUCE

"BREASTS"

Low Calorie

Serves 4

Cooking Time:
1 ¼ Hours

MY CHICKEN SCRATCHES:

_____

_____

_____

_____

_____

4 chicken breasts, skinned and boned
1 tsp. onion powder
1 tsp. pepper
Juice of 1 orange
1 tsp. grated orange rind
¼ tsp. soy sauce
¼ tsp. coriander

Preheat oven to 325 F.
1. Sprinkle chicken breasts with onion powder and pepper.
2. Place in baking dish. Mix remaining ingredients and pour over chicken.
3. Bake, covered, 325 F. for 1 ¼ hours. Serve with sauce.

2 chicken breasts, split, skinned, boned and cubed
1 apple cut up
1 green pepper, cut up
4 fresh mushrooms, sliced
1 onion, cut up
1 zucchini, sliced
1 tsp. poultry seasoning
1 tsp. onion powder
1 tsp. garlic powder
1 egg, beaten
1 rye cracker, crushed
½ cup chicken broth

Preheat oven to 350 F.

1. Alternate chicken and vegetables on 4 skewers and season with spices.
2. Dip in beaten egg and roll in cracker crumbs.
3. Bake in a covered dish with chicken broth in 350 F. oven for 1 ½ hours.

CHICKEN KABOBS

"BREASTS"

Low Calorie

Serves 4

**Cooking Time:
1 ½ Hours**

MY CHICKEN SCRATCHES:

_____

_____

_____

_____

_____

CHICKEN ON A DIET

"PARTS 'N PIECES"

Low Calorie

Serves 4

**Cooking Time:
1 Hour**

MY CHICKEN SCRATCHES:

_____
_____
_____
_____
_____

1 chicken, cut up
Salt and pepper, to taste
1 can diet orange soda
¼ cup soy sauce

Preheat oven to 325 F.
1. Wash chicken (remove skin) and dry on paper towels.
2. Salt and pepper and place in foil lined broiler pan.
3. Mix together the orange soda and soy sauce and pour over the chicken.
4. Bake 325 F. for 1 hour, basting several times, until tender.

3 chicken breasts, skinned and boned
4 tbsp. soy sauce
1 tbsp. salad oil
1 can unsweetened pineapple juice (1 pt.)
4 tbsp. cornstarch
1 can diet pineapple chunks (8 oz.)
2 cans sliced mushrooms (4 oz. ea.)
1 pkg. frozen peas, thawed (10 oz.)
1 head Chinese cabbage, shredded
3 cups rice, cooked

1. Slice chicken into long thin strips. Dip chicken in soy sauce and brown quickly in oil in large frying pan.
2. Stir just enough pineapple juice into cornstarch to make a paste. Stir in remaining juice and pineapple chunks and mushrooms with liquid into chicken in pan. Heat to boiling.
3. Stir in cornstarch mixture and cook, stirring constantly, until sauce thickens and boil for 3 minutes. Cover, simmer for 15 minutes.
4. Stir in peas. Arrange cabbage on top. Cover and cook 8 minutes longer or until vegetables are tender. Serve over hot rice.

CHINESE CHICKEN

"BREASTS"

Low Calorie

Serves 6

**Cooking time:
50 Minutes**

MY CHICKEN SCRATCHES:

_____

_____

_____

_____

_____

LADY FINGER CHICKEN

"BREASTS"

Low Calorie

Serves 1

**Preparation Time:
30 Minutes
Cooking Time:
45 Minutes**

MY CHICKEN SCRATCHES:

_____
_____
_____
_____
_____

1 ⅓ tsp. diet margarine
1 ½ tsp. chives
1 slice bread
1 chicken breast, skinned and boned
2 tbsp. skim milk

Preheat oven to 375 F.
1. Combine margarine and chives. Roll into finger shape, about 2 x ¼". Chill in freezer for 30 minutes.
2. Put bread in blender and run at medium speed to make fine crumbs.
3. Spread crumbs in an even layer in shallow baking pan. Bake 350 F. for 6 minutes or until crumbs are brown.
4. Flatten chicken to ⅛" thickness. Place margarine "finger" on long side of chicken breast. Roll lightly, folding in sides. Secure with toothpicks.
5. Pour milk into a small bowl. Dip rolled breast in milk, then in crumbs. Repeat. Sprinkle with any remaining milk or crumbs.
6. Place in casserole and bake at 375 F. for 45 minutes. Serve immediately.

Dieters Motto
If at first you don"t recede
diet again!

4 chicken breasts
4 rye crackers, broken in small pieces
5 tbsp. onion, minced
4 tbsp. celery, minced
1 ½ cups mushrooms, cooked and chopped
2 tsp. sage
Salt and pepper
4 tbsp. water

Preheat oven to 350 F.
1. Wash chicken thoroughly.
2. Mix crackers, onion, celery, mushrooms, seasoning and water.
3. Stuff breasts and place in baking dish.
4. Bake, uncovered, 350 F. for 30 minutes. Cover and bake 30 minutes more.

MUSHROOM STUFFED CHICKEN

"BREASTS"

Low Calorie

Serves 4

Cooking Time: 1 Hour

MY CHICKEN SCRATCHES:

PEACH OF A CHICKEN
"BREASTS LEGS & THIGHS"

Low Calorie

Serves 6

**Cooking Time:
1 Hour 5 Minutes**

MY CHICKEN SCRATCHES:

_____

_____

_____

_____

_____

3 chicken breasts, split
3 chicken drumsticks
3 chicken thighs
1 can diet peach halves (1 lb.)
3 tbsp. lemon juice
1 ½ tsp. soy sauce

You little ole" peach, you

Preheat oven to 400 F.
1. Place chicken in single layer in shallow baking dish. Drain and reserve peach syrup. Add lemon juice and soy sauce to syrup. Brush half on chicken.
2. Bake 400 F. for 1 hour or until tender, brushing every 15 minutes with remaining sauce. Place peach halves around chicken. Brush with pan juices and bake 5 minutes longer.

3 chicken breasts, split and skinned
¼ cup orange juice
2 tsp. orange peel, grated
2 tbsp. soy sauce
½ tsp. cinnamon
½ tsp. curry powder
¼ tsp. pepper

1. Wash and dry chicken breasts; place in baking dish.
2. Combine remaining ingredients and pour over chicken. Cover and refrigerate about 2 hours, basting several times. Drain and reserve marinade.
3. Broil chicken until crisp and brown and turn to brown the other side.
4. Heat marinade to serve over chicken or hot cooked rice.

The Best exercise for losing weight..Pushing yourself away from the table.

"BREASTS"

Low Calorie

Serves 3 - 5
**Preparation Time:
2 Hours
Cooking Time:
30 Minutes**

MY CHICKEN SCRATCHES:

_____
_____
_____
_____
_____

TERIYAKI CHICKEN

"BREASTS"

Low Calorie

Serves 4

**Preparation Time:
4 Hours
Cooking Time:
45 Minutes**

MY CHICKEN SCRATCHES:

_____

_____

_____

_____

_____

¾ cup water
1 tbsp. soy sauce
No-calorie sweetener to taste
1 clove garlic, minced
½ tsp. powdered ginger
4 chicken breasts, skinned and boned

1. Put water, soy sauce, sweetener, garlic and ginger in a large saucepan and bring to a boil. Add breasts and simmer 30 minutes or until tender. Do not over cook.
2. Remove from heat and cool, uncovered. Refrigerate at least 4 hours or up to 2 days, covered tightly.
3. Serve cold or reheat in marinade.

1 chicken, cut up and skinned
1 can crushed pineapple, undrained (8 ¼ oz.)
1 envelope dry onion soup mix (1 ½ oz.)
¼ cup apricot jam
¼ cup barbecue sauce

1. Place chicken pieces in a 8x12" baking dish. Cover with waxed paper. Microwave on High for 20 - 22 minutes or until fork tender. Drain off excess grease.
2. Mix together remaining ingredients. Pour over cooked chicken pieces. Cover. Microwave on Medium-High for 6 - 8 minutes or until heated through.

Give a Little,

Get a Little

A LITTLE SWEET 'N SOUR

"PARTS 'N PIECES"

Microwave

Serves 6 - 8

Cooking Time: 30 Minutes

MY CHICKEN SCRATCHES:

_____
_____
_____
_____
_____

BEE STING CHICKEN WINGS

"WINGS"

Microwave

Makes 24 Pieces

Cooking Time: 15 Minutes

MY CHICKEN SCRATCHES:

_____

_____

_____

_____

_____

12 chicken wings
¾ cup molasses or honey
½ - ¾ tsp. cayenne pepper
1 cup shredded coconut

1. Trim off the wing tips and cut apart the two remaining sections of the wings. Coat the pieces with molasses or honey. Sprinkle with cayenne pepper and coconut.
2. Place the pieces on a glass serving platter and cover. Micro-cook on High for about 8 - 10 minutes or until the center pieces are done.
3. Remove the covering and place under the broiler until the skin is crispy.

Note: By cooking first in the microwave, you will avoid having the wings dry out.

1 chicken, whole
Dash of salt and pepper
2 medium apples, quartered, peeled and cored
2 medium oranges, peeled and sectioned
¼ cup orange marmalade

1. Season inside of chicken with salt and pepper. Fill with apples and oranges. Truss. Place chicken, breast side down, on a glass trivet in a baking dish. Shield wing and leg tips with brown paper. Brush with half the marmalade. Cover with waxed paper.
2. Microwave on Medium-High (70%) for 35 - 40 minutes or until fork tender. Turn chicken breast side up halfway through cooking and remove shields. Brush with remaining marmalade. Allow to stand 10 to 15 minutes before serving.

Microwave

Serves 4 - 6

Cooking Time:
1 Hour

MY CHICKEN SCRATCHES:

_____

_____

_____

_____

_____

INDIVIDUAL CHICKEN PIES

"PARTS 'N PIECES"

Microwave

Serves 4

**Cooking Time:
30 Minutes**

MY CHICKEN SCRATCHES:

_____

_____

_____

_____

_____

Pastry for 1 crust pie
1 pkg. frozen mixed vegetables (10 oz.)
⅓ cup onion, chopped
3 tbsp. butter
¼ cup flour
1 tsp. salt
1 ½ cups chicken broth
¾ cup milk
2 cups chicken, cooked and cubed

1. Roll prepared pastry to ¼ inch thick. Cut it to fit the tops of four 10 oz. custard cups or individual pie dishes. Prick several times. Set aside.
2. Place frozen vegetables in a 1 quart casserole. Cover with a tight fitting lid or plastic wrap. Microwave on High for 6 - 8 minutes or until heated through. Drain, and set aside. Place onion and butter in a 2 quart casserole. Microwave on High for 3 - 4 minutes or until onion is tender. Stir halfway through cooking.
3. Stir in flour and salt until smooth. Slowly add broth and milk. Microwave on High for 6 - 8 minutes or until thickened.
4. Add chicken and vegetables. Pour into custard cups or dishes and place pastry over filling. Microwave on High for 6 - 8 minutes or until crust is dry and blistery.

2 cups chicken, cooked and diced
1 can tomato juice (32 oz.)
1 cup cabbage, shredded
1 cup carrots
½ cup corn
2 tbsp. dried minced onion
1 tsp. basil
1 tsp. dried parsley
½ tsp. oregano
¼ tsp. salt
Dash of pepper

1. Combine all ingredients in a 2 quart casserole. Cover with a tight fitting lid or plastic wrap. Microwave on High for 8 - 10 minutes or until boiling. Stir occasionally.
2. Microwave on Medium for 1 hour 10 minutes to 1 hour 15 minutes or until vegetables are soft.

ITALIAN CHICKEN STEW

"PARTS 'N PIECES"

Microwave

Serves 4 - 6

Cooking Time: 1 ½ Hours

MY CHICKEN SCRATCHES:

_____

_____

_____

_____

_____

STUFFED CHICK

"PARTS 'N PIECES"

Microwave

Serves 4

**Cooking Time:
30 Minutes**

MY CHICKEN SCRATCHES:

_____

_____

_____

_____

_____

¼ cup butter
1 chicken, cut up
1 pkg. croutons (5 oz.)
1 cup chicken broth
¼ cup onion, chopped
½ cup celery, chopped
½ tsp. ground sage
½ tsp. poultry seasoning
½ tsp. pepper
Paprika

1. Place butter in a measuring cup. Microwave on High for 45 seconds to 1 minute or until melted. Arrange chicken pieces, thicker pieces toward the outside, in a 8x12" baking dish. Brush butter over chicken. Cover with waxed paper. Microwave on High for 20 - 22 minutes or until fork tender.
2. Remove chicken pieces, set aside. Remove drippings from dish. Combine croutons, chicken broth, onion, celery, sage, poultry seasonings and pepper. Place in baking dish. Arrange chicken pieces over dressing. Sprinkle with paprika. Cover.
3. Microwave on High for 6 - 8 minutes or until heated through. Allow to stand 5 minutes before serving.

½ cup soy sauce
¼ cup cooking oil
1 tbsp. brown sugar
1 tbsp. sherry
1 tsp. garlic powder
¼ tsp. ground ginger
1 chicken, cut up

It's hard to say "No" to more

1. Mix together all ingredients, except chicken in 9x13" dish. Add chicken and coat with sauce.
2. Marinate for at least 30 minutes or overnight in the refrigerator. Drain off most of the sauce. Cover with waxed paper. Microwave on High for 20 - 22 minutes or until fork tender.
3. Turn the chicken over and brush with drippings halfway through cooking. Allow to stand 5 minutes before serving.

TIMELY TERIYAKI CHICKEN

"PARTS 'N PIECES"

Microwave

Serves 4 - 6

**Preparation Time:
30 Minutes
Cooking Time:
22 Minutes**

MY CHICKEN SCRATCHES:

_____

_____

_____

_____

_____

_____

YAM STUFFED CHICKEN

"WHOLE"

Microwave

Serves 4 - 6

Cooking Time:
50 Minutes

MY CHICKEN SCRATCHES:

_____

_____

_____

_____

_____

½ lb. bulk pork sausage
½ cup onion, chopped
½ cup celery, chopped
1 can cooked yams, drained (16 oz.)
2 cups seasoned bread cubes
1 tbsp. parsley
½ tsp. salt
¼ tsp. pepper
1 chicken, whole (4 lbs.)
¼ cup butter

If at first you don't succeed, try reading the directions

1. Place sausage in a 2 quart casserole. Microwave on High for 3 - 4 minutes or until sausage is slightly pink. Add onion and celery to sausage. Microwave on High for 3 - 4 minutes or until tender. Drain off excess grease.
2. Stir in yams, bread cubes and seasonings. Fill chicken with stuffing, breast side down, on glass trivet in a baking dish. (Shield leg and wing tips with brown paper).
3. Brush with half the melted butter. Cover with waxed paper. Microwave on Medium-High for 35 - 40 minutes or until fork tender.
4. Turn breast side up, remove shields and brush with remaining butter halfway through cooking. Allow to stand 10 - 15 minutes before serving.

Left Over But
Not Left Out . . .
(PRECOOKED)

⅓ cup herb seasoned croutons, crushed
¼ cup walnuts or pecans, chopped
1 pkg. cream cheese, softened (3 oz.)
¾ tsp. lemon and pepper seasoning
2 tbsp. butter, softened
1 cup chicken, cooked and diced
1 can crescent dinner rolls

Preheat oven to 350 F.
1. Combine croutons and nuts and set aside.
2. Combine cream cheese, seasoning and butter. Mix well. Add chicken.
3. Separate rolls into 8 triangles. Spread each with chicken mixture. Coat with crumb and nut mixture.
4. Place on greased cookie sheet. Bake at 350 F. for 15-20 minutes until brown.
5. Serve with gravy made from chicken broth. (See Dixie Gravy page 152).

This recipe can be used as an appetizer by cutting each triangle in half and follow the above directions.

A LA' CHICKEN CRESCENTS

Precooked

Serves 2

Cooking Time: 20 Minutes

MY CHICKEN SCRATCHES:

ALL-IN-ONE-CHICKEN-QUICHE

Precooked

Serves 6

**Cooking Time:
45 Minutes**

MY CHICKEN SCRATCHES:

_____

_____

_____

_____

1 ½ cups milk
½ cup biscuit mix
6 tbsp. butter, softened
3 eggs
1 cup chicken, cooked and diced
2 green onions, chopped
1 can sliced mushrooms, drained (4 oz.)
1 cup grated sharp Cheddar cheese

Preheat oven to 350 F.
1. Combine first 4 ingredients in blender and mix well. Turn into ungreased deep 9" or regular 10" pie plate.
2. Add chicken, poking into batter. Top with onion, mushrooms and cheese. Bake at 350 F. until top is golden brown, about 45 minutes.
3. Let stand 10 minutes before serving.

who ate all the quiche??

2 cups chicken, cooked and diced
1 cup almonds, slivered
6 eggs, hard cooked and sliced
2 cups celery, diced
2 cups rice, cooked
2 cups cream of chicken soup
2 tsp. lemon juice
½ tsp. salt
1 ½ cups mayonnaise
1 small onion, grated

Preheat oven to 375 F.
1. Combine chicken, almonds, eggs, celery and rice. Mix slightly and set aside.
2. Mix soup, lemon juice, salt, mayonnaise and onion together.
3. In buttered 3 quart casserole, place one layer of chicken mixture, then a layer of cream sauce. Repeat layers and top with crushed crisp cereal, crackers or potato chips.
4. Bake 375 F. for 45 minutes.

I ate the whole thing

ALMOND CHICKEN with CREAM SAUCE

Precooked

Serves 12

**Cooking Time:
45 Minutes**

MY CHICKEN SCRATCHES:

_____

_____

_____

_____

_____

FLAKY CHICK

Precooked

Serves 4 - 6

Cooking Time:
20 Minutes

MY CHICKEN SCRATCHES:

_____

_____

_____

_____

_____

1 pkg. frozen chopped spinach, cooked and drained, (10 oz.)

2 cups chicken, cooked and diced
or 2 cans boned chicken, drained (5 oz. ea.)

3 hard boiled eggs, chopped

½ cup dill pickle, finely chopped

⅓ cup celery, finely chopped

1 can refrigerated crescent rolls (8 oz.)

¼ cup butter

¼ tsp. dry mustard

1 cup sour cream

2 tbsp. dill pickle juice

Preheat oven to 350 F.

1. In large bowl, combine spinach, chicken, eggs, pickle and celery. Unroll rolls and separate the two rectangles of dough. Place rectangles side by side so long sides overlap ½" then press or roll the dough to form 9x12" rectangles.

2. Combine butter, melted with dry mustard and brush over dough.

3. Spread half chicken over dough to within 1" of edges. Starting at long side, roll up and pinch ends to seal. Place seam down on greased sheet. Repeat second roll. Cut 2" diagonal slashes at 2" intervals across the top.

4. Bake 350 F. for 18-20 minutes until deep golden brown. Cool slightly. Place on serving plate.

5. For the sauce, combine the sour cream and pickle juice and serve over the chicken rolls.

½ cup milk
½ tsp. salt
1 can cream of mushroom soup (10½ oz.)
1 can chop suey vegetables (14 oz.)
2 pkgs. frozen french style green beans, thawed (9 oz.)
3 cups chicken, cooked and diced
⅓ cup onion, chopped
1 ½ cups Cheddar cheese, cubed or grated
1 can french fried onions, (3½ oz.)

For the king of the hill

Preheat oven to 350 F.
1. Stir milk and salt into soup until smooth.
2. Drain chop suey vegetables. Fold into soup, along with green beans, chicken and onion. Add cheese.
3. Spoon mix into 8"x12" baking dish. Bake 350 F. for 45 minutes or until beans are tender.
4. Remove from oven and top with french fried onions and return to oven for about 10 minutes. Allow to stand 10 minutes before serving.

JOLLY GIANT CHICKEN

Precooked

Serves 6 - 8

Cooking Time: 55 Minutes

MY CHICKEN SCRATCHES:

_____

_____

_____

_____

_____

MEXICAN MUFFIN DIVAN

Precooked

Serves 6

**Cooking Time:
15 Minutes**

MY CHICKEN SCRATCHES:

_____

_____

_____

_____

_____

2 cups chicken, cooked and diced
1 cup mushrooms, sliced
⅓ cup picante sauce
¼ cup mayonnaise
4 tbsp. green onions, sliced
4 tbsp. green chilies, chopped
3 English muffins, split and toasted
1 cup broccoli, cooked and chopped
6 extra-thick slices pasteurized process cheese, cut in half

Preheat oven to 350 F.

1. Combine chicken, mushrooms, picante sauce, mayonnaise, onions and chilies.
2. Mix lightly. Spoon equal portions on muffin halves. Top with broccoli.
3. Bake on ungreased cookie sheet 350 F. for 10 minutes.
4. Top each with a slice of cheese and continue to bake until cheese just begins to melt.

Makes 6 open face sandwiches.

1 can cream of chicken soup (10 ½ oz.)
1 cup chicken, cooked and diced or 1 can boned chicken
  (5 oz.)
2 tsp. minced onion
⅓ cup milk
1 cup noodles, cooked
1 cup green beans, cooked
Buttered bread crumbs

Preheat oven to 400 F.
1. Blend all ingredients, except bread crumbs.
    Put in 9x13" baking dish.
2. Top with bread crumbs.
3. Bake 400 F. for 25 minutes.

More cluck for your buck

NOODLES CASSEROLE

Precooked

Serves 4

**Cooking Time:
25 Minutes**

MY CHICKEN SCRATCHES:

_____

_____

_____

_____

_____

SCALLOPED CHICKEN

Precooked

Serves 6 - 8

Cooking Time:
30 Minutes

MY CHICKEN SCRATCHES:

_____

_____

_____

_____

1 ½ tbsp. butter or margarine
⅓ cup slivered almonds
1 envelope onion-mushroom soup mix
1 tbsp. flour
2 cups milk
2 cups potatoes, cooked and sliced
2 cup chicken, cooked and diced
2 cups carrots, cooked and sliced

Good Family Dish!

Preheat oven to 350 F.

1. In medium saucepan, melt butter and saute almonds. Stir in soup mix blended with flour and milk. Bring to a boil, then simmer, stirring constantly until sauce is slightly thickened, about 5 minutes.
2. In a greased 1 ½ quart casserole, layer potatoes, chicken and carrots, plus half the sauce. Repeat with another cup of potatoes, chicken and carrots and top with remaining sauce.
3. Bake 350 F. for 30 minutes or until heated through.

Too hot to handle

3 tbsp. butter
1 large onion, chopped
1 ½ cups canned tomatoes
1 green pepper, chopped
1 cup canned okra
2 tbsp. rice
4 - 5 cups chicken stock made with whole chicken
Salt and pepper
2 cups chicken, cooked and diced
1 tbsp. parsley
1 ½ tsp. tarragon
¾ cup corn, cooked
Croutons

1. Melt butter in soup pot. Cook onion 5 - 6 minutes, covered until tender not brown. Add tomatoes, green pepper, okra and rice. Pour in stock. Mix well.
2. Cover pan, simmer until vegetables are tender, 20 - 30 minutes. Add chicken, seasoning and corn. Reheat. Serve hot with croutons.

CHICKEN GUMBO

"PARTS 'N PIECES"

Soups & Salads

Serves 4

**Cooking Time:
40 Minutes**

MY CHICKEN SCRATCHES:

CHICKEN STEW

"PARTS 'N PIECES"

Soups & Salads

Serves 6 - 8

Cooking Time:
3 Hours

MY CHICKEN SCRATCHES:

½ cup cooking oil
1 chicken, cut up
Salt and pepper
Flour
3 onions, chopped
3 tomatoes, peeled and quartered
8 green olives
1 bay leaf
½ tsp. mixed herbs
Chicken broth
1 cup mushrooms, sliced

*Give a booster
to your rooster.
To your chicken,
a delight*

1. Heat oil in large pan. Coat chicken pieces with salt, pepper and flour. Brown on all sides. Remove chicken from pan.
2. Add onions and tomatoes. Fry 5 minutes. Add olives, bay leaf and herbs. Sprinkle with 2 tbsp. flour. Mix well. Replace chicken and enough broth to cover. Cover and simmer for 2 - 2 ½ hours until chicken is tender.
3. Add mushrooms. Remove bay leaf. Put chicken on large serving plate. Arrange vegetables around chicken.
4. Thicken broth with flour. Season and pour some over chicken. Serve remaining separately.

4 cups chicken broth
2 cups celery, finely chopped
1 clove garlic, pressed
1 cup half and half
Salt and pepper
2 cups chicken, cooked and diced
¾ cup Parmesan cheese, grated

Some like it Hot!!

1. Pour broth into large saucepan. Boil and add celery and garlic. Simmer 10 minutes or until tender. Pour into blender and process until pureed.
2. Return to saucepan. Add half and half, salt and pepper and bring just to boiling.
3. Stir in chicken and cheese. Heat, stirring until cheese is melted and soup well blended.

CREAM OF CHICKEN SOUP

"PARTS 'N PIECES"

Soups & Salads

Serves 8

Cooking Time: 30 Minutes

MY CHICKEN SCRATCHES:

GRANDMA'S CHICKEN NOODLE SOUP

"PARTS 'N PIECES"

Soups & Salads

Serves 6

**Cooking Time:
1 ½ Hours**

MY CHICKEN SCRATCHES:

_____

_____

_____

_____

_____

1 chicken, cut up
½ tsp. salt
Water to cover
1 cup carrots, sliced
1 ½ cup celery, chopped with leaves
½ cup onion, chopped
¾ tsp. poultry seasoning
1 tbsp. parsley flakes
2 cups noodles, uncooked

1. Simmer chicken in salted water in covered saucepan until tender, approximately 1 hour. Remove chicken from broth and cool. Remove skin and bones and dice chicken.
2. Skim off fat from broth. Measure broth and add water, if needed to make 5 cups. Boil and add chicken, vegetables and poultry seasoning. Simmer, covered, 20 minutes.
3. Add parsley and noodles, simmer uncovered 10 minutes or until noodles are tender.

6 cups chicken broth
1 chicken breast, split
¼ lb. vermicelli
⅓ cup vegetable oil
1 large tomato, peeled and chopped
1 ripe avocado
3 hot green chilies, chopped
Salt and pepper

1. Boil broth in large saucepan. Add chicken, reduce heat to low and simmer 25 minutes. Remove and cool chicken.
2. Skin, remove bones and shred chicken. Break vermicelli into 2 inch pieces.
3. Heat oil in large skillet and lightly brown vermicelli. Drain on paper towel.
4. Heat broth to boiling. Add vermicelli and cook until tender. Add tomato and chicken. Heat thoroughly.
5. Peel and cut avocado into chunks and add to soup along with chilies, salt and pepper. Heat thoroughly.

Hot Stuff

MY CHICKEN SCRATCHES:

_____
_____
_____
_____
_____
_____

CALIFORNIA CHICKEN SALAD

"PARTS 'N PIECES"

Soups & Salads

Serves 4
**Preparation Time:
2 Hours
Cooking Time:
10 Minutes**

MY CHICKEN SCRATCHES:

_____

_____

_____

_____

_____

½ cup water
¼ tsp. salt
½ cup instant rice
2 ¼ cups frozen broccoli, corn and
  red pepper, cooked and drained
2 cups chicken, cooked and diced
½ - ¾ cup mayonnaise
¾ tsp. curry powder
¼ tsp. pepper
2 ripe avocados

1. Bring water and salt to a boil in a 2 quart saucepan. Stir in rice. Cover, remove from heat and let stand 5 minutes.
2. Add vegetables, chicken, mayonnaise, curry powder and pepper. Toss to blend. Chill.
3. Just before serving, cut avocados in half. Remove pit and peel. Spoon ¼ of the vegetable mixture into each half.

4 cups chicken, cooked and diced
2 cups celery, diced
3 tbsp. lemon juice
Salt and pepper
½ cup dairy sour cream
½ cup mayonnaise
1 ½ tsp. curry powder
4 eggs, hard boiled and chopped
2 eggs, hard boiled and sliced
Parsley

1. Toss chicken, celery, lemon juice, salt and pepper. Mix in sour cream, mayonnaise and curry powder. Carefully fold in chopped eggs.
2. Cover and chill. Just before serving, spoon chicken mixture into lettuce cups. Garnish with egg slices and parsley.

Love "Em and Leaf "Em

CHICKEN CURRY SALAD

"PARTS 'N PIECES"

Soups & Salads

Serves 12

**Preparation Time:
2 Hours**

MY CHICKEN SCRATCHES:

_____

_____

_____

_____

_____

CHILLED POULET de MENTHE CHICKEN SALAD

"BREASTS"

Soups & Salads

Serves 4

Preparation Time:
2 Hours
Cooking Time:
25 Minutes

MY CHICKEN SCRATCHES:

_____

_____

_____

_____

2 tbsp. dried mint leaves
2 chicken breasts, skinned and boned
1 can chicken broth, undiluted and fat skimmed (10 oz.)
1 tbsp. lemon juice
2 scallions, sliced

Dressing:
1 clove garlic, minced
½ cup plain lowfat yogurt
2 tbsp. lemon juice
Salt and pepper
1 tbsp. mint leaves
Paprika

Poulet it again, Sam...

1. Put 2 tbsp. mint leaves in bottom of pan. Add chicken breasts, chicken broth and water to cover. Simmer very low until cooked through, 20 - 25 minutes. Cool.
2. Slice chicken into thin strips. Toss with 1 tbsp. lemon juice and scallions. Chill.

To make dressing:
Combine garlic, yogurt, lemon juice, salt and pepper and 1 tbsp. mint leaves. Chill. At serving time, arrange chicken on lettuce and top with yogurt mixture. Sprinkle with paprika. Garnish with cucumber and tomato.

1 ½ cups chicken, cooked and diced
1 cup fresh mushrooms, sliced
1 cup skim milk
1 medium apple, cored and diced
¼ medium pineapple, peeled, cored, diced
½ cup chicken bouillon
½ tsp. salt
½ tsp. paprika
½ tsp. onion powder
2 cups shredded raw spinach
Nutmeg, to garnish

1. Combine all ingredients, except the spinach and nutmeg in saucepan. Cook over low heat, stirring frequently for 10 minutes, or until mushrooms are translucent.
2. Divide spinach evenly into 2 individual bowls. Pour half the chicken mixture over each portion of spinach. Sprinkle with nutmeg.

Serves 2

**Cooking Time:
15 Minutes**

MY CHICKEN SCRATCHES:

_____

_____

_____

_____

_____

JELLIED CHICKEN SALAD

"PARTS 'N PIECES"

Soups & Salads

Serves 4

**Preparation Time:
2 Hours
Cooking Time:
5 Minutes**

MY CHICKEN SCRATCHES:

_____

_____

_____

_____

_____

1 envelope unflavored gelatin
1 ¾ cups chicken broth
2 cups chicken, cooked and diced
2 tbsp. lemon juice
¼ cup celery, chopped
2 tbsp. pimento-stuffed olives, sliced
1 tbsp. onion, minced
¼ tsp. salt
Pimento
Tomato wedges

Cool it, Honey!!

1. Sprinkle gelatin in ½ cup chicken broth to soften. Stir over low heat until gelatin is dissolved. Stir in remaining broth.
2. Chill until slightly thickened. Stir chicken, lemon juice, celery, olives, onion and salt into gelatin. Pour into loaf pan, 9"x5"x3". Chill until firm. Garnish with pimento and tomato wedges.

1 chicken breast, split
4 tbsp. soy sauce
Boiling water
¾ lb. fresh bean sprouts
1 carrot, pared and shredded
1 cup slivered green onions and tops
3 tbsp. minced parsley
¼ cup white vinegar
2 tsp. sugar
½ cup blanched slivered almonds, toasted

1. Simmer chicken in mixture of 1 tbsp. soy sauce and 2 cups water in covered saucepan 15 minutes, or until chicken is tender. Pour boiling water over bean sprouts. Drain; rinse under cold water to cool and drain thoroughly.
2. Remove chicken and cool. Skin and bone chicken; shred chicken into large bowl. Add bean sprouts, carrot, green onions and parsley.
3. Blend vinegar, sugar and remaining soy sauce, stirring until sugar dissolves. Pour over chicken and vegetables; toss to coat all ingredients. Cover and refrigerate 1 hour. Just before serving, add almonds and toss to combine.

MANDARIN CHICKEN SALAD

"BREASTS"

Soups & Salads

Serves 6
**Preparation Time:
1 Hour
Cooking Time:
15 Minutes**

MY CHICKEN SCRATCHES:

_____

_____

_____

_____

_____

TWO SALAD DRESSINGS

Makes
1 to 2 cups
each

MY CHICKEN SCRATCHES:

_____

_____

_____

_____

_____

YOGURT HONEY DRESSING

1 container plain low-fat yogurt (8 oz.)
½ cup low calorie mayonnaise
2 tbsp. honey
1 tbsp. lemon or lime juice
⅛ tsp. salt

1. In small bowl, whisk together all ingredients until well blended. Cover and refrigerate.

CHILLED CHICKEN SALAD DRESSING

1 clove garlic, minced
1 cup plain lowfat yogurt
3 tbsp. lemon juice
salt and pepper
1 tbsp. mint leaves
paprika

1. Combine garlic, yogurt, lemon juice, salt and pepper and mint leaves. Chill.

Come Up And See Me Sometime...

(SPECIAL OCCASION)

1 cup toasted almonds
½ cup grated Parmesan cheese
1 tsp. garlic salt
1 tsp. poultry seasoning
1 tsp. paprika
½ tsp. dillweed
½ tsp. pepper
Lemon juice
3 chicken breasts, split and skinned

Preheat oven to 400 F.
1. Grind almonds in blender. Combine with cheese, garlic salt, poultry seasoning, paprika, dillweed and pepper.
2. Dip chicken in lemon juice and coat with almond coating. Place on baking sheet. Bake 400 F. for 45 minutes.

Worth a standing ovation

ALMOND CHICKEN

"BREASTS"

Special Occasion

Serves 3

**Cooking Time:
45 Minutes**

MY CHICKEN SCRATCHES:

_____

_____

_____

_____

_____

CHICKEN CORDON BLEU

"BREASTS"

Special Occasion

Serves 6

Cooking Time:
30 Minutes

MY CHICKEN SCRATCHES:

_____

_____

_____

_____

_____

6 chicken breasts, boned
6 thin slices ham
2 cups Swiss cheese, grated
1 egg
1 ½ tsp. cooking oil
1 tbsp. water
Flour
Bread crumbs

Sauce:
1 medium can crushed
  pineapple, undrained
1 cup brown sugar
1 tbsp. lemon juice
1 tbsp. cornstarch
½ cup water
¼ cup Sherry
4 tbsp. butter

Preheat oven to 325 F.

1. Pound chicken breasts to approximately ¼" thickness (without tearing), top with 1 slice ham, and ⅓ cup Swiss cheese. Roll up carefully, tucking in ends as you roll.
2. Combine egg, cooking oil and water in a small bowl. Roll chicken in flour, then in egg mixture and then in bread crumbs.
3. Place in pan and bake 325 F. for 20 - 25 minutes.
4. While chicken is baking, prepare **Fruit Sauce** by combining pineapple, brown sugar and lemon juice. Cook on medium heat until bubbly; turn down heat to simmer.
5. Add cornstarch with water slowly until slightly thick.
6. Add Sherry and butter. Serve hot over cooked chicken.

6 to 8 chicken breasts
½ cup flour
¼ tsp. garlic salt
½ tsp. paprika
1 tsp. salt
4 tbsp. salad oil or shortening
1 cup chicken broth or dry white table wine
2 cups pitted cherries
½ cup (or more) brandy

Look Out Honey, Here It Comes!

Preheat oven to 375 F.

1. Shake chicken breasts in paper bag with flour, garlic salt, paprika and salt.
2. Fry slowly to a rich, golden brown in hot salad oil.
3. Arrange in flame proof baking dish and add wine or broth. Cover and bake at 375 F. for 20 minutes.
4. Remove cover and add cherries. Return to oven and bake, uncovered, 15 - 20 minutes longer or until chicken is tender. Place on top of range, pour on brandy, heat on low heat long enough to warm the brandy (do not allow to boil) and then set aflame. When brandy stops burning, serve chicken with the cherries and sauce.

CHICKEN JUBILEE

"BREASTS"

Special Occasion

Serves 6 - 8

**Cooking Time:
1 Hour**

MY CHICKEN SCRATCHES:

CHICKEN WITH CAPERS & OLIVES

"BREASTS"

Special Occasion

Serves 4

Cooking Time: 30 Minutes

MY CHICKEN SCRATCHES:

_____

_____

_____

_____

4 chicken breasts, split, skinned and boned
1 tsp. salt
½ tsp. pepper
16 pitted green olives
1 tbsp. olive oil
1 tbsp. butter
⅓ cup onion, finely chopped
1 tbsp. red vine vinegar
2 cups canned tomatoes, crushed
¼ cup capers, drained
1 bay leaf
½ tsp. dried thyme
3 tbsp. parsley, finely chopped

""Company Pleasers""

1. Cut and trim away any fat from chicken. Sprinkle with salt and pepper. Cut each olive lengthwise into quarters (there should be about ¼ cup).
2. Heat the oil and butter in a heavy skillet. Add the chicken and cook until golden brown on one side, about four minutes. Turn and cook about two minutes. Transfer chicken to a warm dish.
3. Add the onion and cook, stirring until wilted. Add the vinegar and cook, stirring about 10 seconds.
4. Add the tomatoes, olives, capers, bay leaf, and thyme. Bring to a boil and cook about 5 minutes.
5. Remove the bay leaf. Spoon the sauce over the chicken and sprinkle with parsley.

1 cup fresh coconut, grated
1 cup water
1 lemon, peeled and sliced
1 cup onion, chopped
2 tbsp. butter
3 chicken breasts, skinned, boned and diced
½ tsp. ginger
½ tsp. salt
1 canned green chili pepper, sliced
1 tbsp. flour

My "Girls" Just Love This!

1. In a saucepan, combine coconut, water, lemon and onion. Bring to a boil. Remove from heat and strain.
2. Melt butter in a large skillet and add chicken. Cook until chicken turns white. Add ginger, salt and chili pepper.
3. Pour in coconut liquid, cover and simmer for 10 minutes.
4. Mix flour with a small amount of cold water and stir into sauce. Bring to a boil and simmer for 2 minutes.

COCONUT CREAM CHICKEN

"BREASTS"

Special Occasion

Serves 4 - 6

Cooking Time: 30 Minutes

MY CHICKEN SCRATCHES:

_____

_____

_____

_____

_____

139

CORNISH HENS & NOODLES

"CORNISH HENS"

Special Occasion

Serves 6

Cooking Time:
1 ½ Hours

MY CHICKEN SCRATCHES:

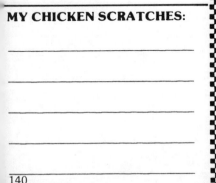

Very Fancy!

6 frozen Cornish Hens (about 1 lb. each) thawed
¼ tsp. salt (per hen)
½ cup buttermilk
2 pkg. seasoned coating mix for chicken
1 pkg. spinach noodles (1 lb.)
¾ tsp. onion salt
3 tbsp. butter

Preheat oven to 350 F.
1. Remove giblets from hens. Rinse and pat dry, inside and out. Sprinkle with salt. Brush hens with buttermilk then shake on coating mix. Place breast side up and not touching on baking sheet.
2. Bake 350 F. for 1 ½ hours or until tender.
3. Cook noodles in a large saucepan as directed on label. Drain and return to saucepan and add onion salt and butter. Toss lightly to mix.
4. Spoon noodles on serving platter and arrange hens on top.

6 large chicken breasts, boned and butterflied
½ cup teriyaki sauce
½ lb. ground pork
⅓ cup bread crumbs
¼ cup milk
2 tbsp. green onions and tops, chopped
2 tbsp. water chestnuts, chopped
1 tbsp. soy sauce
1 egg, beaten
¼ tsp. ginger
⅛ tsp. white pepper
2 tbsp. butter

Fine Fare

Preheat oven to 350 F.

1. Place chicken in large plastic bag and add teriyaki sauce. Seal and marinate in refrigerator for 1 hour.
2. Combine pork, bread crumbs, milk, onions, chestnuts, soy sauce, egg, ginger and pepper. Divide into 6 equal portions. Reserving marinade, remove chicken.
3. Place portion of stuffing mixture on flesh side of each breast. Tuck ends of breasts over stuffing and secure with skewers.
4. Place in baking pan, skin side up. Blend butter and 2 tbsp. marinade. Brush chicken. Bake 350 F. for 1 hour or until brown. Baste frequently. Serve with rice.

EAST WEST CHICKEN

"BREASTS"

Special Occasion

Serves 6

**Preparation Time:
1 Hour
Cooking Time:
1 Hour**

MY CHICKEN SCRATCHES:

_____
_____
_____
_____
_____
_____

FLAMING APRICOT-SAUCE CHICKEN

"WHOLE"

Special Occasion

Serves 4 - 5

Cooking Time:
1 ¾ Hours

MY CHICKEN SCRATCHES:

_____

_____

_____

_____

1 whole chicken
Salt and pepper
2 tbsp. melted butter

Sauce:
½ cup apricot jam
¼ cup light corn syrup
2 tbsp. lemon juice
¼ cup brandy or 1 tbsp. lemon extract

Preheat oven to 375 F.

1. Sprinkle body cavity with salt and pepper. Skewer opening and tie together close to the body. Tuck wings back under body. Place chicken in shallow baking dish. Brush with butter.
2. Bake 375 F. for 1 ½ to 1 ¾ hours or until chicken is well browned and tender. Remove skewers and string and place chicken on serving platter.
3. Combine jam, corn syrup and lemon juice and heat to boiling. In separate pan, warm brandy but do not allow to boil. Pour brandy on top of sauce, ignite and spoon the flaming sauce over the chicken. Serve at once.

2 ½ cups chicken broth
1 cup rice
1 cup plain yogurt
½ cup currants
⅓ cup blanched slivered almonds
½ cup scallions, thinly sliced
½ tsp. ground allspice
6 Cornish game hens (1 ¼ to 1 ½ lbs. each)

Preheat oven to 350 F.

1. Bring broth to a boil in a medium saucepan. Add rice, cover tightly and simmer 20 minutes. Remove from heat. Let stand, covered, until water is absorbed, about 5 minutes.
2. Stir in ½ cup of the yogurt, currants, nuts, scallions and allspice. Stuff hens with rice mixture, using about ½ cup for each hen.
3. Fold wings back, tie legs together. Arrange hens on a rack in a large shallow roasting pan. Brush with ¼ cup yogurt. Bake 350 F. for 30 minutes.
4. Brush hens with the remaining yogurt and continue baking for another 30 minutes.

"OLD-COUNTRY" CORNISH HENS

"CORNISH HENS"

Special Occasion

Serves 6

Cooking Time: 1 ½ Hours

MY CHICKEN SCRATCHES:

_____

_____

_____

_____

_____

REAL CHICKEN CACCIATORE

"BREASTS"

Serves 4

**Cooking Time:
1 Hour**

MY CHICKEN SCRATCHES:

_____

_____

_____

_____

4 chicken breasts, skinned
½ tsp. salt
½ tsp. pepper
1 cup tomato puree
½ cup mushrooms, sliced
¼ cup dehydrated onion flakes
¼ cup celery, chopped
¼ cup pimentos, chopped
1 garlic clove, minced
⅛ tsp. rosemary leaves
Pinch of allspice
1 tbsp. lemon juice
1 tbsp. wine vinegar

Preheat oven to 325 F.
1. Sprinkle chicken with salt and pepper.
2. Brown over high heat in non-stick pan, turning frequently.
3. Transfer to baking dish. Set aside.
4. Combine tomato puree, mushrooms, onion flakes, celery, pimentos, garlic, rosemary and allspice. Cook over low heat for 5 minutes. Stir in lemon juice and wine vinegar.
5. Spoon over each chicken breast. Bake 325 F. for 35 minutes or until chicken is tender. Baste often with sauce during cooking.

1 whole chicken
¼ tsp. salt
½ tsp. pepper
2 tbsp. cooking oil
1 package chicken flavored stuffing mix
1 cup apple, grated
¾ tsp. lemon peel, grated
¼ cup walnuts, chopped
¼ cup raisins
¼ cup celery, finely chopped

Apple glaze:
½ cup apple jelly
1 tbsp. lemon juice
¾ tsp. cinnamon

Preheat oven to 350 F.
1. Sprinkle inside of chicken with salt and pepper. Brush outside with oil. Set aside.
2. In a bowl, combine stuffing mix, grated apple, lemon peel, walnuts, raisins and celery. Mix thoroughly. Place stuffing inside chicken. Place chicken in a baking pan and cover loosely with foil.
3. Bake 350 F. for about 1 hour.
4. In a small saucepan, combine apple jelly, lemon juice and cinnamon. Simmer, stirring constantly, for 3 minutes or until blended. Brush chicken with glaze. Bake, uncovered, 30 minutes longer or until leg moves freely when lifted or twisted. Brush frequently with glaze.

STUFFED CHICKEN with APPLE GLAZE

"WHOLE"

Special Occasion

Serves 4

Cooking Time:
1 ½ Hours

MY CHICKEN SCRATCHES:

_____

_____

_____

_____

_____

145

STUFFED GOURMET BREASTS

"BREASTS"

Special Occasion

Serves 4

**Cooking Time:
1 Hour**

MY CHICKEN SCRATCHES:

_____

_____

_____

_____

_____

4 chicken breasts, skinned and boned
Salt and lemon pepper
½ cup butter
½ tsp. paprika
1 ½ cups mushrooms, sliced
¾ cup celery, sliced
½ cup onion, chopped
1 cup water
3 cups herb-seasoned dry stuffing mix

Eat Your Heart Out, Honey!

Preheat oven to 375 F.

1. Sprinkle chicken lightly with salt and lemon pepper. Melt butter and combine 1 tbsp. of the butter with paprika and brush over chicken.
2. Saute mushrooms, celery and onion in remaining butter until onion is soft. Add water and heat to boiling. Pour over stuffing mix, tossing to moisten evenly. Place in a baking dish and top with chicken.
3. Bake uncovered 375 F. for 1 hour or until chicken is well browned and tender.

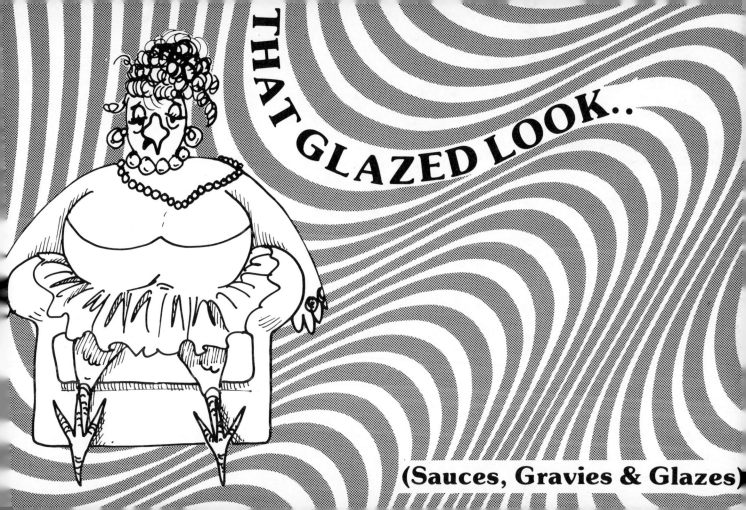

THAT GLAZED LOOK..

(Sauces, Gravies & Glazes)

BARBECUE GLAZE

¼ cup pineapple syrup or juice
½ cup honey
¼ cup margarine, melted
¾ tsp. mace

1. Combine all ingredients and heat to melt and combine thoroughly.
2. Baste chicken with glaze occasionally while cooking.

Makes enough for 1 chicken.

BASIC BARBECUE SAUCE

½ cup onion, chopped
3 tbsp. oil
¼ cup catsup
¼ cup water
¼ cup maple syrup
3 tbsp. wine vinegar
1 tbsp. Worcestershire sauce

1. Saute onion in oil in a small skillet.
2. Add all ingredients and simmer 15 minutes, stirring occasionally.
3. Use as a baste for chicken the last 15 - 20 minutes of cooking.

Makes enough for 1 chicken.

DIPPING SAUCE

¼ cup soy sauce
¼ cup sherry or sake
2 tbsp. sugar

1. Combine all ingredients in saucepan.
2. Heat until sugar dissolves.

Makes ⅔ cups.

ALMOND CHICKEN COATING

1 cup toasted almonds
½ cup grated Parmesan cheese
1 tsp. garlic salt
1 tsp. poultry seasoning
1 tsp. paprika
½ tsp. dillweed
½ tsp. pepper
Lemon juice

1. Grind almonds in blender.
2. Combine with cheese, garlic salt, poultry seasonin
   paprika, dillweed and pepper. Coating may be
   stored in air tight container in dry cool location.
3. Dip chicken in lemon juice and coat with
   almond coating before baking.

Makes enough for 1 chicken.

CREOLE SAUCE

1 can tomatoes, undrained (16 oz.)
1 onion, chopped
1 green pepper, chopped
1 cup celery, chopped
1 can mushrooms, undrained (4 oz.)
2 tbsp. dried parsley
1 tsp. oregano
1 tbsp. Worcestershire sauce

1. Combine all ingredients and mix well.
2. Spoon over chicken before baking.

Makes enough for 1 chicken.

APPLE GLAZE

½ cup apple jelly
1 tbsp. lemon juice
1 tsp. cinnamon

1. Combine all ingredients in a saucepan. Cook 3 minutes.
2. Brush on chicken before baking.

Makes enough for 1 chicken.

DIXIE GRAVY

½ cup skim milk
½ cup chicken bouillon or broth
1 tsp. onion powder
1 tsp. imitation butter flavoring

1. Combine all ingredients in a small saucepan.
2. Cook over low heat for 5 minutes.
3. Serve over chicken.

Makes enough for 4 pieces of chicken.

LEMON SAUCE

½ cup lemon juice
2 tbsp. grated onion
½ tsp. pepper
¼ cup oil
¼ tsp. salt
½ tsp. thyme
1 clove garlic, crushed

1. Combine all ingredients and mix well.
2. Use as a basting sauce or serve with cooked chicken.

Makes enough for 1 chicken.

MUSHROOM SAUCE

1 can cream of mushroom soup (10 ½ oz.)
3 tbsp. sherry
½ cup Cheddar cheese, grated
¼ cup dehydrated onion

1. Combine all ingredients and mix well.
2. Spoon over chicken before baking.

Makes enough for 6 pieces of chicken.

ORANGE SAUCE

4 tbsp. orange peel, grated
½ cup orange juice
¼ tsp. salt
1 tsp. dry mustard
1 tsp. paprika
¼ tsp. red pepper sauce
⅓ cup salad oil

1. Combine all ingredients and mix well.
2. Pour over chicken before baking.

Makes enough for 1 chicken.

FRUIT BARBECUE SAUCE

1 cup pineapple juice
1 cup orange juice
½ cup catsup
¼ cup honey
2 tbsp. prepared mustard
1 tbsp. butter
1 tsp. salt

1. Simmer all ingredients together for 30 - 40 minutes, until slightly thickened.
2. Use to baste chicken.

Makes enough for 1 chicken.

SOY BASTE

1 cup soy sauce
¼ cup oil
1 tsp. MSG
½ cup sugar
3 tsp. grated ginger
1 clove garlic, crushed

1. Combine all ingredients and heat thoroughly.
2. Use as a baste for chicken the last 30 minutes of cooking.

Makes enough for 1 chicken.

SPICY BASTE

½ cup sherry
4 tbsp. lemon juice
⅓ cup honey
2 tsp. cinnamon

1. Mix together all ingredients. Pour over chicken and refrigerate 4 - 5 hours, turning occasionally.
2. Drain marinade and reserve to baste the last 15 minutes of cooking.

Makes enough for 1 chicken.

TER-YAKI SAUCE

⅔ cup soy sauce
¼ cup white wine
3 tbsp. sugar
½ tsp. ginger
1 clove garlic, chopped

1. Combine all ingredients and mix well.
2. Marinate chicken for 1 hour or more.
3. Baste 2 or 3 times during baking.

Makes enough for 1 chicken.

SWEET SOUR SAUCE

1 can tomato sauce (8 oz.)
¼ cup honey
¼ cup tarragon wine vinegar
1 tbsp. soy sauce
1 tbsp. lemon juice

1. Combine all ingredients and spoon over chicken before baking.

Makes enough for 6 pieces of chicken.

TOMATO SAUCE

1 can tomato sauce (8 oz.)
1 can mushrooms (4 oz.)
2 tbsp. white wine or water
1 tsp. dried garlic
1 tsp. oregano
½ tsp. basil

1. Combine all ingredients and mix well.
2. Spoon over chicken before baking.

Makes enough for 6 pieces of chicken.

**CHICKEN
KNOWLEDGE**

(How To . . .)

"CHICKEN TIPS"

The main requirement for successful chicken cooking is "low temperature" (325 F.). Regardless of the type of bird, a low temperature cooks the bird more uniformly tender and keeps the meat more juicy.

When pan frying, browning chicken a few pieces at a time in uncrowded skillet helps the batter adhere.

When deep-frying, fry without a basket for better results.

When turning chicken, use tongs rather than a fork. If you make holds in the chicken pieces you will lose the natural juices and it will dry out.

If the chicken is done but looks too pale, rub it with paprika or baste it with drippings and return it to the oven a little longer.

Always clean chicken in cold water.

To test for doneness, move the leg and if the drumstick and thigh joint breaks or moves easily, the chicken is done. The drumstick meat should be very soft when pressed between the fingers.

Substitute two 5 oz. cans or 2 cups diced cooked chicken for 2 whole chicken breasts.

To thaw frozen chicken - leave in original wrapper on plate and allow 24 hours in refrigerator per 5 lbs. of chicken.

To quick thaw - leave in wrapper and put in sink, cover with cold water, changing often and allow ½ hour per pound. **Never** allow poultry to stand at room temperature.

"CHICKEN TIPS"

When preparing chicken, **always** thoroughly wash with soap and hot water the countertop, cutting board, knives or whatever the raw chicken has touched. This will prevent any possibility of bacteria. In addition, do not use the same knife that was used on the raw chicken on any other food unless the knife has been washed.

To check chicken for doneness: pierce chicken with fork - juices should be clear **not** pink.

CALORIE CHART FOR COOKED CHICKEN

Flesh & skin, no bone, broiled - 3 oz.	**185 cal.**
Breast, fried & boned - ½ breast	**215 cal.**
Leg, fried with bone	
(thigh & drumstick) - 4.3 oz.	**245 cal.**
Canned, boneless - 3 oz.	**170 cal.**

How to ...

Dressed Weight	Oven Temp.	Minutes Per Pound	Total Roasting Time
3 ½ to 4 lb.	350 F.	40 - 45	2 to 2 ¾ hrs.
4 to 5 lb.	325 F.	35 - 40	2 ½ to 3 hrs.
5 to 6 lb.	325 F.	30 - 35	3 to 3 ½ hrs.

Average Weight	Type of Chicken	Serving Per Person	Cooking Method
1 to 2 ½ lb.	Broiler	¼ to ½ bird	Broil, Fry, Roast
2 ½ to 3 ½ lb.	Fryer	¾ to 1 lb.	Fry, Roast
Over 3 lb.	Roaster	½ to ¾ lb.	Fry, Roast
4 lb. & Over	Capon	½ to ¾ lb.	Roast
2 ½ to 5 ½ lb.	Pullet	½ to ¾ lb.	Fry, Roast, Braise
Any Weight	Fowl-Hen	¼ to ¾ lb.	Braise, Steam, Stew
3 to 6 lb.	Cock-Rooster	¼ to ¾ lb.	Simmer-Soup

161

"CHICKEN COOKING METHODS"

BROILED CHICKEN

Place broiling rack about 6 inches from source of heat, so that the top of the chicken will be about 4 inches from the heat. (This gives a temperature of about 350 F. at surface of chicken.)

BRAISED CHICKEN

Brown pieces of chicken slowly, uncovered, on all sides in hot oil over medium heat. Use a heavy iron or aluminum skillet that can be tightly covered. The slow browning of all pieces not only develops a rich brown color in the chicken and gravy but contributes a delicious flavor to the finished chicken. The browning should take about ½ hour. Add ¼ cup of water or other liquid, cover tightly and simmer over low heat until chicken is tender.

FRIED CHICKEN

Coat chicken pieces with seasoned flour. Heat enough cooking oil to make a layer of ¼ inch deep. Fry slowly until browned on both sides (about 30 minutes); reduce to low heat, cover, continue to cook very slowly until tender; turning occasionally to brown evenly.

OVEN FRIED CHICKEN

Prepare same as "Fried". When pieces are delicately browned, transfer to a roasting pan with a tight-fitting cover. Pour the drippings from the skillet over the chicken and add 2 to 4 tbsp. of water, cover and bake in moderately slow oven until tender.

CHICKEN COOKING METHODS

ROAST CHICKEN

Use a pan of the smallest possible size to hold the bird so that the drippings will not be spread too thin. (This prevents burning.) Place breast down on wire rack in roasting pan, brush with melted butter. When cooking time is half over, turn chicken on back and brush again with melted butter.

STEAMED CHICKEN

Use a large roasting chicken, leave whole and place in the upper part of a steamer. Have about 3 cups of water rapidly boiling in the botton, cover tightly and boil water gently until tender.

STEWED CHICKEN

Use a 3 ½ to 5 lb. stewing, roasting chicken or pullet. Cut into serving pieces or leave whole. Fit pieces into kettle with a tight fitting cover. Barely cover with cold water and add salt. Vegetables may be added for flavor. Cover, heat to boiling, then reduce heat and simmer gently until tender.

BONING CHICKEN BREAST

Place breast, skin side down, on a cutting surface. Turn the breast so that the pointed tip is away from you. In the center of the cleavage of the wishbone end, that is facing you, is a little tip of white cartilage, cut through it. Press fingers against the edge of the breast bone. Bend it back until the bone snaps loose. Work fingers down in between meat and bone and lift out entire bone, including the cartilage at pointed end. Extending back from each of the two rib cages toward the point are two long thin bones. Slide the tip of the knife under one of these bones, loosening it. Lift out and turn breast around to enable you to lift out the other long bone and the wishbone.

CUTTING UP WHOLE CHICKEN

Place chicken on its back on cutting surface, grasp one leg and lift it away from the body and cut through the skin all the way through the joint close to the back. Repeat with the other leg. If you bend the leg and thigh together toward the center, you will see the knee joint. Cut through the leg joint to separate the thigh from the drumstick. Pull wing from the body, cut on the inside of the wing, through the joint. Repeat on the other wing. Separate the breast from the back in one large piece by cutting along the ribs on each side.

Chicken for frying is usually cut into 11 pieces: 2 drumsticks, 2 thighs, 2 wings, 2 pieces of back - the tail and rib piece, 2 pieces of breast - one with the wishbone and the other with the heel bone. and the neck, which for frying should be cut off with the skin attached. If more pieces of breast meat are desired, the 2 large breast pieces may be cut in half. In cutting up the chicken, be sure that the skin belonging to each piece is left attached, both for better appearance when cooked and in order that the layer of fat immediately under the skin may be present to give flavor to the meat. If you are counting calories, remove the skin.

To test for doneness, move the leg and if the drumstick and thigh joint breaks or moves easily, the chicken is done. The drumstick meat should be very soft when pressed between the fingers.

CARVING CHICKEN

Let the cooked chicken set out at room temperature for 15 - 30 minutes before carving so that you do not lose all the juice from the bird. Place chicken on carving surface, breast side up. Holding end of the leg nearest you, bend it downward while you cut through the thigh joint to separate thigh from the body. Cut leg at the joint to separate the thigh and drumstick. Insert the fork into the breast and carve the wings off as close to the body as possible. Carve the meat starting at the tip of the breastbone and cut down toward the wing joint. Repeat on the other side of the chicken.

"CHICKEN TIPS"
SPICES THAT COMPLIMENT CHICKEN

Barbecue Seasoning
Bay leaf
Celery - Flakes, Salt & Seed
Cloves
Curry Powder
Garlic - Liquid, Salt & Powder
Ginger
Marjoram
Nutmeg
Onion - Minced, Powder & Salt
Oregano

Paprika
Parsley Flakes
Pepper - Ground Black, Whole Black, Crushed Red, Ground Red & Ground White
Poultry Seasoning
Rosemary
Saffron
Savory - Leaf & Herb
Tarragon
Thyme

METRIC CONVERSION CHART

Tsp. and Tbsp. Liquid or Dry	Cup (8 oz.) Liquid or Dry
1/4 tsp. = 1/5 mill	1/4 cup = 60 mill
1/2 tsp. = 3 mill	1/3 cup = 80 mill
1 tsp. = 5 mill	1/2 cup = 125 mill
3 tsp. = 15 mill	3/4 cup = 190 mill

Cup (10 oz.)
Brittain uses a
10 oz. cup
Liquid or Dry

1/4 cup = 80 mill
1/3 cup = 100 mill
1/2 cup = 150 mill
3/4 cup = 230 mill
1 cup   = 300 mill

EQUIVALENTS

3 tsp.	= 1 tbsp.
1 fluid ounce	= 2 tbsp.
1/4 cup	= 4 tbsp.
1/3 cup	= 5 tbsp. plus 1 tsp.
1 cup	= 1/2 pint
2 cups	= 1 pint
4 cups	= 1 quart
4 quarts	= 1 gallon (liquid)
8 quarts	= 1 peck (dry)
16 ounces	= 1 pound
3 small eggs	= 2 large eggs
1/4 pound butter	= 1/2 cup
1 pound shortening	= 2 1/2 cups
1 medium lemon	= 3 tbsp. juice
1 medium orange	= 6 - 8 tbsp. juice
1 grated orange rind	= 1 tbsp.

"EZ TO FIND INDEX"

This Is It
Chicken Lovers!